The
Great Reunion

by

John David Whitehead

Also included...
A Road That Won't Travel

Copyright © 2004 by John David Whitehead

All rights reserved

Second Edition, November 2004

Prestige Publishing
PO Box 15243, North Little Rock, AR 72231

Printed in the United States of America
by Prestige Press, Inc. of North Little Rock, AR 72117

Book Design by *Ron Oberlag*
Cover Art by *Arts & Ideas Studio*
Edited by *Mike Howard and Gail Oberlag*

Request for permission to reprint material
from this work should be sent to Prestige Publishing

Library of Congress Cataloging-in-Publication Data

Whitehead, John David, 1935 -
The Great Reunion
160 p. : ill.; 22 cm.

Library of Congress Control Number: 2004111743

ISBN: 0-9740208-7-7

A Road That Won't Travel

The Author
John David Whitehead

Dedication

This book is dedicated to Farrell Clements in honor of his bringing the Word of **God** to the Fort Worth Medical Center, as a Federal Inmate. He came preaching the gospel and helping men come back to the realization that our **Lord** and **Savior** is a lot more important than any amount of time spent in this life.

"**His** is eternal", ours is very temporary.

Thank You, Farrell ...

Special Recognition

There are many who have helped carry me through this life. But there are some very special ones that I want to give special recognition who have done more than what was asked of them.

§ § §

First, I want to thank Barbara for the forty-four years of marriage. Next I want to thank my sons David and Doyen and my daughter Donna for always holding fast and loving me

§ § §

I want to give special thanks to my three brothers Jim, Marvin, and Danny and my sister Betty. Thank you for the patience you have had.

§ § §

I could go on and on giving thanks to a great many more. But most of all I want to say thank you **Father** for giving me your **Son, Jesus Christ** and for the **Comforter** he sent to me from heaven, **The Holy Ghost**.

-- John David Whitehead

Contents

Purpose of this book 7

Part 1, *The Great Reunion* 9

Part 2, New Testament 87

A Road That Won't Travel... 117

Forward 119

Introduction 147

Five Steps to Salvation......... 147

Notes................................. 151

The Purpose of This Book

Just as **God** appeared and spoke to Moses from the burning bush, and as Moses drew near with curiosity to see why the bush wasn't consumed with fire, **God** spoke to him and said, "Take off your shoes for you are standing on Holy Ground." (Exodus 3:5)

It is with this book, The Great Reunion, that I hope to give you assurance that after **God** spoke to Moses and enlightened him of the things he wanted Moses to do, that you also see the purpose **God** had for choosing Moses. It is commonly accepted that Moses wrote the first five books of the Bible – Genesis, Exodus, Leviticus, Numbers and Deuteronomy.

God wanted to communicate with his people while they were wandering around in the wilderness. He wanted to give them instructions on how to live their lives and to depend on Him in order to live a more abundant life. He chose Moses as that instrument. Moses kept records and instructed **God**'s people as **God** instructed Moses. **God** had a plan. He gave Moses the Ten Commandments and the instructions on how to build the Ark of the Tabernacle. **God** gave his people instructions how to sacrifice to Him using animals to represent the blood of the "Lamb of **God**" who He would send as the final sacrifice for our sins so we could have eternal life and join Him in that *"Great Reunion"*.

All of the scriptures are taken from The King James version which was translated into the English language by fifty-four **Holy Spirit**-filled men approximately four hundred years ago. It came to be known as "**God's** Holy Word"- the Bible. Let the Holy Bible be your burning bush. It was written for that purpose for all men, women and children. So fall in love with it.

In His Service Always,
    -- John David Whitehead

The Great Reunion

Part 1
The Great Reunion

The Great Reunion

Chapter 1

In the beginning **God** created the heaven and the earth. Now through my own curiosity I ask myself, "How long ago was this?" My spirit answers that question, "No man knows." And again my spirit tells me for sure **God** was even before that creation.

I believe that after the creation of heaven and earth **God** the **Father**, **God** the **Son** and the **Holy Ghost** stood on a hill of Glory looking at what had been created. And **God** was not with satisfaction at what He had created. **God** is never with satisfaction until everything is in perfect order, as He wants it to be.

Going to the Holy Bible, **God** saw there was total darkness over His creation and seeing that total darkness He was not satisfied. So He said (Genesis 1:3) *"Let there be light:' and there was light."* Then in the next verse *(Genesis 1:4) "And **God** saw the light, and that it was good: and **God** divided the light from the darkness."*

For the next six days **God** created each and everything that gave Him pleasure, but after all of his creating, He still wasn't satisfied and even though **God** saw that what He had created was good, **God** said (Genesis 1:26) *"Let us make man in our image, after our likeness: and let them have dominion over the fish of the sea, and over the fowl of the air, and over the cattle, and over all the earth, and over every creeping thing."*

I do believe at that very time, the **Son** turned and looked at His **Father** and said, "Everything you do is done unto perfection, that will mean you will have to create man to perfection and you will have to give him a perfect will to be righteous or evil." So **God** said to His **Son**, "Yes I know, and I also know that man will be persuaded to do evil, and not do the thing I command him to do." At that time, I believe the **Son** saw that this man would be created and was to be eternal joy and never leaving **God** the **Father** without this permanent joy. Man would be created to live forever, eternally and for always.

Try to understand, when "**God**" does anything, that thing must be done to perfection. That's just the way **God** does things. So the **Son** was right when He said, If you create man in our imagine he will be created to perfection; he will be perfect in every way – in looks, form, and a perfect will. I would think that Adam was the most handsome man that has ever been. And I would think that Eve was the most beautiful woman that has ever been on earth. I would think that after Adam and Eve had eaten of the tree of forbidden fruit, Adam looked and saw Eve in a very different way. He probably noticed that Eve's body was not the same form as his and was looking at her with a lustful eye and with a desire in his heart for her. This different way of looking at Eve was brand new.

I believe that every man, woman, or child that **God** has allowed to be created in the womb of a woman, by the seed of a man are all created equal in spirit, equal in faith, and equal in love. Sometimes we get into that pity-party and start thinking why is it that **God** never does anything for me? Or we will say **God** never talks to me.

A Road That Won't Travel

Well, my answer to that statement is, "Are you reading His Holy Word, the Bible?" That is how **God** will speak to any and all of His children.

There is no telling how many people have been killed in order to bring this Holy Word, the Bible, to you. If you are reading his Holy Word, then read more.

My Dear Reader, read for yourself out of the Bible; do not take any man's word whether it be this author or a great well known preacher's word. It would be risking too much to take someone's word for what the Bible says; your very soul is at stake in what it says. Read your Bible for knowledge, wisdom and most importantly for Salvation. (Rescue from great danger).

Right now this very minute, The **Comforter** is speaking to the ears of my heart saying, "Tell your readers if they will read *The Great Reunion* with an open mind and a prayerful heart, and go to each and every scripture written in this book, with **God's** Holy Book right beside it to back up each and every scripture reading for themselves, I will speak what **God** wants to say to this person before they finish and complete the reading of this book."

This is a pretty strong statement, huh? But right now the **Comforter** is saying, "Trust me. Try me. Believe without a doubt that it will come to pass."

Now let us go back into this great story of **God's** creating man and woman, Adam and Eve.

The Great Reunion

Chapter 2

I believe that **God** the **Father**, the **Son**, and the **Holy Ghost** all came into an agreement: that after man would do his own thing by that perfect will **God** had given him, he would fall and choose to do evil. These three Godheads made their own plan right then. The **Son** saying, "I will be willing to leave my place of Paradise in this Heaven and go down to earth and live as a man for thirty three years. After thirty three years, I'll go to a cross and spill my blood as a sacrifice as payment for man's sin."

I believe that at that very time, the **Holy Ghost** said to the **Father**, "Because of the great pleasure and love you will have with man, and after the **Son** has gone down to the created earth that man has lived on and has spent thirty three years as a man knowing the difference between good and evil, He will stand as an example for men to live by. He will be a lamb without blemish and will become a sacrifice and die on a tree for the sins of man in order to bring men back to you, **Father**, in perfect harmony once again. And then as the man **Jesus** comes back to the paradise of heaven and once again stands at your right hand, **Father**, I will then be willing at His command and by your work to go down to the ones who are of a "holy spirit" and live with them in their holy soul with their holy spirit as their **Comforter**. By the great power given to them by my coming, they will accept **Jesus** as their only salvation. I will provide the great power to heal and do the great miracles that men will do."

I believe that this agreement became as ONE

ACCORD between these three Godheads at this very time even before **God** formed man from the dust of the ground and breathed into his nostrils the breath of life and man became a living soul.

Genesis 2:8 *"And the **Lord God** planted a garden eastward in Eden; and there He put the man whom He had formed."*

The Bible doesn't say how long Adam lived before **God** looked at Adam and commanded *"Of every tree of the garden thou may freely eat: But of the tree of knowledge of good and evil, thou shall not eat of it; for in the day that thou eat thereof, thou shalt surely die."* (Genesis 2:16-17)

I am sure that Adam's question even at that time was, "What is to die?" You see many Christian believers think that **God** said this to Adam and Eve both. But Adam told Eve what **God** had said to him. Because at the time **God** told Adam this, Eve had not yet been taken from Adam's side. In Genesis 2:18 *"And the **Lord God** said, 'It is not good that man should be alone; I will make a helpmate for him."*

*"And the **Lord God** caused a deep sleep to fall upon Adam and he slept: and He took one of Adam's ribs and closed up the flesh instead thereof."* (Genesis 2:21)

Isn't it wonderful when we see and realize **God** loves us so much He wants us to have every good? He is always thinking of things we need and things that will make us happy. **God** will still do it for us if we will let Him.

I'm sure when **God** brought the woman to Adam they walked around in the garden with Adam showing her the whole garden. As they came to the tree that is in the midst of the garden Adam told the woman, whom He had named Eve, what the **Lord** had said and that they were not to eat of the fruit in the midst of the garden or they would surely die.

I believe that **God** had made a covenant with Adam not to eat of that tree; and that **God** would give him everything he wanted and would allow him to live forever and eternally.

But Eve did eat of the tree being coached into it by the serpent who asked, *"Has **God** not said if thou eat of this tree that thou would surely die? Thou shall not surely die."*

That was the first lie that was given to a human being. I am sure Eve, after believing that lie and seeing that the fruit was good, turned to Adam and said, "Come on Adam, it's good." Then Adam himself was persuaded to eat also.

Naturally **God** came to fellowship with Adam and Eve. (Genesis 3:9) *"And the **Lord God** called unto Adam and said unto him, 'Where are Thou?'"*

You see **God** knew where Adam and Eve both were even before He called and asked, "Where Are Thou?"

Dear Reader, I want to stop long enough to tell you that **God** the **Father**, **Jesus** the **Son**, and the **Holy Ghost** all three know exactly where you are and also if you are involved in sin. This Trinity knows all about that sin. No sin can be hid from these three who are keeping record.

In the New Testament if you will look in 1 John 5:7, The Bible says, *"For there are three that bear record in* *heaven, the **Father**, the **Word**, and the **Holy Ghost**, and these three are one."* That's enough of altar calling for now. But do look at it yourself.

Now going back to Adam as he said in Genesis 3:10. *"I heard thy voice in the garden and I was afraid because I was naked; and I hid myself."* Adam had now broken the covenant that **God** had made with him. The first thing Adam did was to try and hide his sin by blaming Eve. (Genesis 3:12) *"And the man said, 'The woman whom thou gave to be with me, she gave me of the tree and I did eat."*

Eve just the same as said, "The Devil made me do it!" In Genesis 3:13 the word says *"And the **Lord God** said unto the woman, 'What is this that thou hast done?' And the woman said, 'The serpent beguiled me and I did eat."* Too many times we sin and cover up that sin by blaming others whereas if we would just own up and confess that sin with a broken and contrite heart, **God** would look at **Jesus** and say, I forgive.

We, just like Adam, always want to do things our way. And that won't work. **God** had his own plan for men. But Adam and Eve jumped the gun and got in front of that plan that **God** had. We as men and women most of the time look at the situation that is in front of us and say or think, "Oh, I can handle this with no problems." What happens most of the time is that ole hill of a problem turns into a mountain all because we were saying secretly to ourselves, "This is so small I don't want to bother **God** with this."

Go to the New Testament and read what **Jesus** said. (John 14:16) *"And I will pray the **Father** and He shall* *give you another* **Comforter** *(*with a capitol C*) that He may abide (*Live*) with you forever."* Now read John 14:26 where **Jesus** again said, *"But the* **Comforter** *(*again with a capitol C*), which is the* **Holy Ghost,** *whom the* **Father** *will send in my name, He shall teach you all things, and bring all things to your remembrance whatsoever I have said unto you."*

Now read Luke 24:49: *"And behold, I send the promise of my* **Father** *upon you: but tarry ye in the city of Jerusalem, until ye be endued (received) with power from on high."* The "Power" is the **Holy Ghost!**

This Power is all the while saying to you, "Let me help. I will show you the answer". But we humans, having our stubborn ways, refuse to listen. Instead we are saying, "No, I can do it." Until this molehill turns into a mountain, we never realize we should have listened. Then we want to cry out to **God** saying, "**Lord**, help me!" And He will. Why? Because, He loves you.

Now let us go back to the man *Adam.* Have you ever really thought of the heartbreaks and sorrows this sin brought upon Adam? (Genesis 3: 17-19) *"And unto Adam He said, 'Because thou hast hearkened unto the voice of thy wife, and hast eaten of the tree of which I commanded thee saying, 'Thou shalt not eat of it': cursed is the ground for thy sake; in sorrow shalt thou eat of it all the days of thy life."*

"Thorns also and thistles, shall it bring forth to thee; and thou shalt eat of the herb of the field."

"In the sweat of thy face shalt thou eat bread till thou return unto the ground; for out of it wast thou taken; for dust thou art, and unto dust shalt thou return."

The Great Reunion

And, if this was not enough, Adam and his wife Eve came together and Eve conceived and had a son, Cain. And again they went together and Eve conceived again and brought forth Cain's brother, Abel. Adam and Eve loved them both dearly.

The heartbreak of Adam's sin would not stop at the cursing of the ground. Eve, having conceived by Adam's seed, gave birth to these two brothers, Cain and Abel.

Then the sin of jealousy entered Cain and he murdered his brother Abel in a fit of rage. (Genesis 4:8) *"And Cain talked with Abel his brother; and it came to pass, when they were in the field, that Cain raised up against Abel his brother and slew him."*

This was be the first murder in the history of man's creation. What a heart break it must have been for these parents, Adam and Eve, to have a son who murdered his own brother. How horrible this sin was.

The Bible doesn't say how many children Adam and Eve had, it only speaks of one more other than Cain and Abel. (Genesis 4:25) *"And Adam knew his wife again; and she bare a son, and called his name Seth, for **God**, said she hath appointed me another seed instead of Abel, whom Cain slew."*

Adam was one hundred and thirty years old when he begat Seth. The Bible doesn't say what his age was when he begat Cain and Abel. But it does say that after he begat Seth he lived another eight hundred years and that Adam begat sons and daughters. The Bible doesn't give Eve's age when she died, nor does it say anything else about Eve conceiving again. The Bible just says Adam begat sons and daughters. So we know there were other children begotten by Adam in these eight hundred years after Seth was born.

Now, after the sin Adam committed of eating from the tree of forbidden fruit, he did live to a ripe old age of nine hundred and thirty years. (Genesis 5:5) *"And all the days that Adam lived were nine hundred and thirty years: and he died."*

The Great Reunion

Chapter 3

During the thousands of years that man lived on the earth they multiplied, living long lives and having many children. And it did come to pass that the earth's population grew and men and women became full of wickedness and great were their sins doing evil to the fullness of their imagination.

Does this sound like the ways of today? Making wars, murdering, stealing, lying, committing adultery and divorce, unbelief, doubting, false worship, having other gods before the true ONE and ONLY **GOD**! Yes, it does sound like today's world.

Now what did **God** do about the sins of those times? (Genesis 6:6) *"And it did repented the **Lord** (made Him sorry) that He had made man on the earth, and it grieved Him at His heart."* At that time **God** was so disappointed with man that He said in Genesis 6:7 *"And the **Lord** said, 'I will destroy man whom I have created from the face of the earth; both man and beast, and the creeping thing and the fowls of the air; for it repenteth me(* made me sorry) *that I have made them."* I don't believe that **God** was talking to himself, but with his **Son** and the **Holy Ghost**.

But as **God** looked down on earth He remembered poor Noah. And **God,** being full of grace and mercy looked at Noah and saw His grace that was in Noah. The grace **God** had given to himself.

So, with His love for Noah, **God** revealed to Noah His plan to destroy all of flesh upon the earth. (Genesis 6:8) *"But Noah found grace in the eyes of the **Lord**."*

The Great Reunion

(Genesis 6:13) *"And **God** said unto Noah, 'The end of all flesh is come before me; for the earth is filled with violence through them; and, behold, I will destroy them with the earth."*

God had had enough of man's evil ways and what he was saying is "I'm through with these people." Then he looked at Noah and must have thought, "But I'm not through with you Noah. So you and your sons must build an Ark and get ready because I am going to cause it to rain and flood all of the earth and destroy all flesh that has breath; everything upon the earth."

I'm sure Noah must have asked, "What is rain, **God**?" At this time it had never rained before. **God** had caused water as dew to come up from the ground and watered the earth this way.

God even had to give Noah the diagram to build the Ark. (Genesis 6:15) *"And this is the fashion that thou shalt make it of: The length of the ark shall be three hundred cubits* (about 450 feet) *and the breath of it fifty cubits (*about 75 feet) *and the height of it thirty cubits* (about 45 feet)." It was to be three stories inside. Noah started building the Ark right away as **God** had commanded. And he built on it for about 100 years.

Can you imagine how terrible this must have been on Noah and his family mentally? Having all the people come out to where he and his family were working on the Ark and the people jeering and laughing at Noah and his family saying, "How high is the dew today, Noah?" For a man or woman to torment a person is awfully hard to take. But to have his family taunted also must have been almost unbearable. But remember Noah was **God**'s man.

A Road That Won't Travel

I sometimes wonder what the people thought when they saw the beasts (animals) coming to the Ark and going into the Ark two by two. Surely, they must have thought, "How strange, something must be going to happen." And when the rain from heaven started (as it never had rained on earth before since the creation of man) they must have said, "What's this? Is this what Noah was predicting when he told us to get ready that a flood was coming?" Noah did warn them. I'm sure they probably became very frightened.

The Bible says that Noah did according to all that **God** commanded him. He took two of every flesh (male and female) that were not clean beasts and seven each of male and female that were clean beasts. Noah took more of the clean beasts into the Ark because he would use them for sacrificing. He took all food that is eaten by both man and beasts into the Ark. Then when the rain started the Bible says **God** shut the Ark's door.

(Genesis 7:11-12) *"In the six hundredth year of Noah's life, the second month, the seventeenth day of the month, the same day were all fountains of the great deep broken up and the windows of heaven were opened. And the rain was upon the earth forty days and forty nights."*

All flesh that was not in the Ark and that remained on the earth died during the forty days and forty nights that it rained. The water from the rain covered the highest mountains. (Genesis 7:19-20) *"And the waters prevailed exceedingly upon the earth; and all the high hills that were under the whole heaven, were covered. Fifteen cubits upward did the waters prevail; and the mountains were covered."* Can you even imagine such rain? That is twenty-two feet over the highest rise.

After that time, the rain stopped. (Genesis 7:24) *"And the waters prevailed upon the earth a hundred and fifty days."* But during the next 14 months or so, Noah and his family stayed in the Ark until **God** spoke unto Noah telling him to leave the Ark and take his family and all the flesh out of the Ark with him.

What would you think was the first thing this righteous man Noah did upon leaving the Ark? My Bible says (Genesis 8:20) *"And Noah built an altar unto the **Lord**; and took of every clean beast, and of every clean fowl, and offered burnt offerings on the altar."* That was the first thing.

The altar would also become **God's** earthly meeting place, his home on earth. **God** made His covenant with man through Noah to be forever. (Genesis 9:11) *"And I will establish my covenant with you, neither shall all flesh be cut off any more by the waters of a flood; neither shall there any more be a flood to destroy the earth."*

You can rest assured that never again would water destroy the earth. Be assured of this. (Genesis 9:13-14) *"I do set my bow in the cloud, and it shall be for a token of a covenant between me and the earth. And it shall be in the cloud; and I will look upon it that I may remember the everlasting covenant between **God** and every living creature of all flesh that is upon the earth."*

And Noah lived after the flood three hundred and fifty years. This was one of **God's** other gifts - old age. (Genesis 9:28 -29) *"And all of the days of Noah were nine hundred and fifty years and he died."*

Chapter 4

Now the whole earth at this time was of one language and as men again started to multiply they started leaving **God** out of their lives and doing things their way. (Genesis 11:4) *"And they said, 'Go to, let us build us a city and a tower, whose top may reach unto heaven; and let us make us a name, lest we be scattered abroad upon the face of the whole earth."* This would be the construction of the Tower of Babel. But that tower would never be finished because **God** would not allow it to be. Here again, man was trying to build his own way to heaven.

Does this sound familiar looking at today's world travels first the moon, next all the planets and finally heaven itself? But **God** will not allow this either.

Here is what **God** did to the people who were trying to build this Tower of Babel. (Genesis 11:7) *"Go to, 'Let us* (more than one) *go down, and there confound their language that they may not understand one another's speech."*

This turned into probably more than a dozen different languages. All of which were brand new. So they had to stop their building of the tower. **God** always has His way of stopping what He doesn't want. But His love and mercy is forever saying, "Stop this sin you have that is against Me." **God** is saying to you now, "You need to cast this sin away. You need to stop it now!" So then do it.

God at this time had His eye and hand on another man and that man was Abram, the son of Terah who was seventy years old at the time Abram was born. As

The Great Reunion

Abram grew into manhood he took to wife Sarai; who had no children to give to Abram. (Genesis 11:30) *"And Sarai was barren; she had no child."*

(Genesis 12:1) *"Now the **Lord** had said unto Abram, Get thee out of thy country, and from thy kindred, and from thy father's house, unto a land that I will show thee."*

Abram, having faith that **God** was going to show him a land as **God** promised, left his homeland. But from the first, he left being out of agreement with **God**. For **God** had said to leave all of your kindred behind. Probably Abram said to himself, my father is old and I'm all Lot has. So Abram took his father Terah, and his nephew Lot and Sarai, Abram's wife, and left the land of Ur of the Chaldees, to go into the land of Canaan. When they came into the land of Haran, they stopped and dwelt there. The Bible doesn't say how long they dwelt there or why; maybe because Terah was so old. Remember he was seventy when Abram was born and now he is one hundred forty five and Abram is seventy-five. (Genesis 12:4) *"So Abram departed, as the **Lord** had spoken unto him; and Lot went with him and Abram was seventy and five years old when he departed out of Haran."*

What Abram was saying as far as **God** was concerned was, "I don't trust **God** to take care of Lot. I need to do it myself." Look what Abram got by going against **God** and doing it himself. Lot turned out to be the biggest thorn of all in Abram's side. So **God** same as said, "O.K. Abram, go ahead and do it your way." This sounds kind of like me.

A Road That Won't Travel

So Abram departed from Haran as **God** had spoken and journeyed on into the land of Canaan. There was a famine in the land so Abram passed through the land further south to Egypt to live temporarily until the famine had passed.

Now Abram knew that his wife Sarai was very beautiful and fair to look at. So he said to her, *"When the Egyptians see thee, that they shall say, this is his wife; and they will kill me, but they will save thee alive."* (Genesis 12:12) That brought on one of the very few lies that Abram would tell. But the two of them, Abram and Sarai, made up this lie for Sarai to say, "I am his sister."

Sarai was so beautiful, even at the age of 65, that her beauty was told to Pharaoh, and he did bring Sarai into his house. But from the first hour that she was there, things started happening. *"And the **Lord** plagued Pharaoh and his house with great plagues because of Sarai, Abram's wife."* (Genesis 12:17)

Pharaoh finally got wind that his troubles started immediately after Sarai came into his house. He must have confronted her telling her to give him every detail of her past. Sarai probably said to Pharaoh, "Even though the truth was true when I said I am Abram's sister, for I am his half sister, but also I'm his wife."

At that time Pharaoh must have shook with fear because he had to have known that Abram was a most Godly man. And the Egyptians were, at that time, covered with a moral law that must have said "Don't commit adultery with another man's wife." The thought of how close Pharaoh came to breaking that law must have given him the fear of which I speak of. (Genesis 12:19)

"Pharaoh said, Why saith thou, she is my sister? So I might have taken her to me to wife; now therefore behold thy wife, take her and go thy way."

Now during this time Abram traded, worked, and I would imagine conned a little. (Genesis 13:2) *"And Abram was very rich in cattle, silver, and gold."*

Abram got a free escort out of Egypt with the Pharoah's men carrying all his possessions, even herding his cattle and other animals. Why? Because Pharoah feared this man and Abram's **God**. (Genesis 12:20) *"And Pharoah commanded his men concerning him; Abram; and they sent him away, and his wife and all that he had."* Those men were told by Pharoah, "Get him out of Egypt right now with no harm to be done to him." **God** was with Abram.

Now going out of Egypt, Abram had his first confirmation with the thorn in his side (Lot). While looking at the land with the herdsmen of Abram's cattle and the herdsmen of Lot's cattle, strife between the herdsmen began. That will always happen.

(Genesis 13:8-9) *"And Abram said unto Lot, 'Let there be no strife, I pray thee, between thee, and me and between my herdmen and thy herdmen; for we be brethren.* (Abraham was pleading.) *Is not the whole land before thee? Separate thyself, I pray thee, from me; if thou go to the left hand then I'll go to the right, or if thou depart to the right, then I will go to the left."*

Lot looked in all directions and chose to go by the way of the plains of Jordan, that being the best looking of the land. Abram went into the land of Canaan, which at that time looked bad. But still he went into that land.

About 500 years later it would become the land of promise – the land of Milk and Honey for the Jews.

There would be many other hardships on Abram, all because of Lot. **God** knew what he was saying when he said to Abram from the start, "Take no kindred." Yes, **God** knew Lot would be a problem.

God later would show a vision of Abram's seed by saying, "Look at the stars and see how many you can count. Then look at the grains of the sand on the beach and see how many you can count." And the **Lord** said, *"So shall your seed be out of your own bowels, if you will wait upon me."*

Naturally the first thing Abram said was "How can that be?" The **Lord** must have said, "Because I said it." (Genesis 15:6) *"And he believed in the **Lord**; and he counted it to him for righteousness."* Abram believed and had faith that it would come to pass.

You see at this time Abram had no children. And Sarai was barren and as far as both Abram and Sarai were concerned they could not have children. Now they were old and Sarai came up with the solution to the problem. She looked at her servant Hagar whom she brought up out of Egypt. (Genesis 16:2) *"And Sarai said unto Abram, 'Behold now, the **Lord** hath restrained me from bearing: I pray thee, go in unto my maid; it may be that I may obtain children by her.' And Abram hearkened to the voice of Sarai."*

Here they go again getting in front of the **Lord**. Just like we do today when things don't go as quickly as we think they should. And we always must pay for getting in front of **God**. One of the hardest lessons to learn in this

The Great Reunion

life is submit to **God's** time, not ours.

Now after Hagar became pregnant, she began to disrespect and despise Sarai. I would imagine she thought since she was with Abram's child, she no longer should be treated as a servant. Sarai went to Abram with the problem and told him that Hagar now despised her. She was probably asking what to do about the situation.

(Genesis 16:6) *"But Abram said unto Sarai, 'Behold, thy maid is in thy hand; do to her as it pleaseth thee.' And when Sarai dealth hardly with her, she fled from her face."* So Hagar went into the wilderness to be alone and weep.

As Hagar sat by a fountain of water, an Angel of the **Lord** came to her asking, "What is wrong, Hagar?" And as they talked, (Genesis 16:11) *"And the Angel of the **Lord** said unto her, 'Behold, thou art with child, and shalt bear a son , and shalt call his name Ishmael; because the **Lord** hath heard thy affliction."*

Here again without our modern day equipment of foretelling the sex of a child, the Angel of the **Lord** is hitting it right on the nail head, even giving Hagar the name and why that name. Names were very important in those days and had meaning for the future of the child.

(Genesis 16:15-16) *"And Hagar bare Abram a son; and Abram called his son's name, which Hagar bare, Ishmael. And Abram was four-score and six years old (86) when Hagar bare Ishmael to Abram."*

I believe that Abram loved his son, Ishmael, born by Hagar the Egyptian. But that was not what **God** had in mind. Abram jumped the gun again and did it his way. As usual, there is always a penalty to pay when we avoid

God's way and do things our way.

To this very day, there is still turmoil and wars and rumor of wars between the descents of this son of Abram's, and his son Isaac. Ishmael was the son of flesh. Isaac was the promised son. The son **God** spoke of (Genesis 17:19) *"And **God** said, 'Sarah thy wife shall bear thee a son indeed;* (a fact: She will.) *and thou shalt call his name Isaac: and I will establish my covenant with him for an everlasting covenant, and with his seed after him."* Now the covenant between **God** and Abram had already been made before this.

(Genesis 17:10-11) *"This is my covenant, which ye shall keep, between me and you and thy seed after thee; every man-child among you shall be circumcised. And ye shall circumcise the flesh of your foreskin; and it shall be a token of the covenant betwixt me and you.*

Abram's name was at this time changed to Abraham. And Sarai's name was changed to Sarah, changed by the **Almighty God** himself.

The **Lord** visits with Abraham and tells him his wife Sarah will have a son within a year. (Genesis 18:10) *"And He said, 'I will certainly return unto thee according to the time of life; and, lo Sarah they wife shall have a son. And Sarah heard it in the tent door, which was behind him."*

(Genesis 18:11) *"Now Abraham and Sarah were old and well stricken in age; and it ceased to be with Sarah after the manner of women."* Did you get what the **Lord** said in the above verse where he said, I will return unto thee according to the time of life? He is telling them He would restore the life-giving physical conditions of the body to produce a son. **God** knew their physical conditions and that Sarah was past childbearing. But **God** had a covenant with Abraham. And **God** keeps his covenant. He is **God**!

Sarah laughed behind the back of the **Lord**. (Genesis 18:13-14) *"And the **Lord** said unto Abraham, 'Wherefore, did Sarah laugh, saying, Shall I of a surety bear a child, which am old? Is anything too hard for the **Lord**? At the time appointed I will return unto thee, according to the time of life, and Sarah shall bear a son."* Again, **God** is telling Abraham that He will restore the life-giving physical conditions of the body at the appointed time and Sarah will have a son. For the **Lord** plainly says what the time will be even before Sarah has conceived and also what the sex of the baby will be.

Also, during the same visit that the **Lord** had with Abraham, the **Lord** also decided to tell Abraham about His plans to totally destroy Sodom. Naturally Abraham thought to himself, "That's Lot's home." So immediately he began to plead with the **Lord** concerning Lot. So, although Lot was still a thorn in the side of Abraham, he was given relief from the destruction of Sodom. The **Lord** had mercy on Lot due to the reasoning of Abraham.

After Isaac was born to Sarah, she said to Abraham, "Cast this bond woman out and her son." Sarah was jealous of Hagar and her son Ishmael who was fourteen years old. It seems that Sarah had seen Ishmael mock Isaac.

Getting ahead of **God** and not waiting for **God's** time is always a mistake. The penalty is always one that will come back with a heart breaking effect on you, and most of the time your family also. In the case of Abraham's sin of getting ahead of the **Lord,** now he was being torn apart from his son Ishmael.

As I said, continuing today wars are raging concerning the descents of these two half brothers, Ishmael and Isaac - Abraham's two sons.

Once again Abraham's faith would be tested concerning his son Isaac who by now had grown into a teenager. But **God** tempted Abraham when He told him, (Genesis 22:2) *"And He said, 'Take now thy son, thine only son Isaac, whom thou lovest, and get thee into the land of Moriah; and offer him there for a burnt offering upon one of the mountains which I will tell thee of."*

Abraham must have thought to himself, "**God** what about my seed being as the stars and as the grains of sand on the beach?" But Abraham at this time did as **God** had directed, knowing by faith, that **God** would not let him down. Abraham took this thing that **God** had said for him to do all the way, and by faith he was ready to slay his son. Now read (Genesis 11:10) *"And Abraham stretched forth his hand, and took the knife to slay his son."*

What tremendous faith Abraham must have had at this time, because at the very last second the angel of the **Lord** called out in a loud voice. (Genesis 22:12) *"And He said, 'Lay not thine hand upon the lad, neither do thou any thing unto him: for now I know that thou fearest **God**, seeing thou hast not withheld thy son, thine only son from me.*

What **God** was telling Abraham was the son of flesh you would have given, as you did in sending him away with his mother Hagar. But this son, the only son that I promised you, who was your only son of the promise of multiplying your son's seed as the stars, and the grain of the beach of the sea, you have not withheld from me.

So **God** was pleased with Abraham for his show of faith. Now read (Hebrews 11:6) in the New Testament, which says, *"But without faith it is impossible to please Him: for he that cometh to **God** must believe that He is, and that He is a rewarder of them that diligently seek Him."*

I can guarantee and promise you if you will listen and diligently seek him, **God** always says to you, "Trust Me. I will do it." In order to build your faith, you must let **God** talk to you. You may say, "How do I do that?" Well, let me tell you. <u>Read your Bible</u>. That is how **God** talks to His children in today's world. It will work! It will bring the desire of your heart. (Read Mark 11:24) (Mark 11:22) *"Therefore I say unto you, 'What things so ever ye desire when ye pray, believe that ye receive them, and ye shall have them."* Have faith in **God**.

Keep in mind a person who has doubt and unbelief in what they are asking for in prayer is not going to receive it until they cast that doubt and unbelief away from them. By saying, "**Father**, I am praying according to your will. I have not asked for anything that you say I want you to have, so according to my faith, I believe it shall come to pass, and I shall have it. Amen."

Chapter 5

Let me tell you this truth. We all are given the same amount of faith. (Romans 12:3) *"For I say through the grace given unto me,* (unmerited favor of **God Almighty**) *to every man that is among you, not to think of himself more highly than he ought to think; but to think soberly, according as **God** hath dealt to every man the measure of faith."*

Yes, **God** did give you and I the same amount of faith that He gave Abraham, Isaac, Jacob, Moses and all of the twelve apostles of **Jesus**. Also **God** gave us the same amount of faith He gave **Jesus** himself. If the measure of faith had been unequal in men, this would not have been fair to men, with one having a portion above what others had. And our **God** is not an unfair **God**.

Now here is the beautiful part, **Jesus,** more than any other, was able to stand on His faith, knowing that He was pleasing His **Father** in being worthy to go to the cross and die for the sins of **God's** children so they could come to that "Great Reunion" that **God** has had in his plan. Amen. Hallelujah!

The spirit of man is in the exact order as faith is, and is equally given to all men in the mother's womb. Yes, these two are given the same to all men, not to be unequaled. Here is where we sometimes fail when we don't develop our faith and spirit to the point to where we continue in unbelief or doubt. We need to stand fast on what we ask and pray for. **God** will do it!

I am reminded of a time many years ago, my precious

The Great Reunion

daughter, who was then a teenager, came to me as I lay resting and watching TV on the living room couch. She had tears in her eyes as she began to talk to me, telling me of her troubles. One of her teenage friends was getting a car and she wanted me to get her one. As she sat beside the couch persuading me that now was the time for her to have a car, what she didn't know was that her mother and I had been talking about this matter a few weeks before this time.

As I got up off of the couch and went to the restroom to wash my face and hands, she began to cry out loudly saying, "What is wrong with you? Don't you hear what I am saying?" I still never said a word. She began to weep bitterly saying "Daddy, please". I stepped into the kitchen where her mother was working cleaning up and said to her mother, "Come on Sweetie, this is the day we need to go get her a car." I will never forget the look on my daughter's face as I told her mother to get ready and we would go buy her a car.

While I am on that thought, please let me take you to the New Testament to Luke 11:13. *"If we then,* (that's me) *being evil, know how to give good gifts unto your children; how much more shall our* **Heavenly Father** *give the* **Holy Spirit** *to them that ask Him"?* Many Christians do not understand this scripture completely and to the fullest. **Jesus** is at this time saying to the reader: **God** wants to give you His **Holy Spirit** – the **Holy Ghost**. You have the same power that **Jesus** had.

Some may say, "Preacher, that is an awesome statement to make." Well, my answer to that is, "If the scripture says it, I do believe it." Now go to John 14:12

and read, *"Verily, verily,* (means truly, truly) *I say unto you, He that believeth on me, the works that I do shall he do; because I go unto my* **Father***."*

What **Jesus** is saying here is, "That gift my **Father** gave you, sent by Him in my name, it has the power to remove every mountain that comes up before you." Why? Because **Jesus** is right now at the **Father's** right hand side pleading and interceding for you. And the power of heaven is right now, today or tonight, willing and ready to come and live with your spirit in the temple of your holy soul. Amen.

The **Holy Ghost** is the Power of Heaven, come down from heaven to be your **Comforter**. The **Comforter** has been with man ever since **Jesus** left earth to go back to heaven.

Chapter 6

Let us go back to Abraham's life where we find that Abraham was one hundred and thirty-seven years of age when Sarah died at the age of one hundred and twenty-seven years, and at that time Isaac was thirty-seven. Isaac was still not married and mourned deeply for his mother. Abraham seeing the deep mourning that was upon his son Isaac, called upon the eldest servant of Abraham's house and said to him, "My son Isaac is in great mourning over the death of his mother Sarah. I am sending you unto my country of my birth and unto my kindred. (Genesis 24:4) *"But thou shalt go unto my country, and to my kindred, and take a wife unto my* son Isaac: *The servant left and went."*

When this servant arrived at his destination he did not take the first woman he came to. This servant prayed to **God** for a sign so he would know whom **God** had chosen for Isaac. This sign would be when the servant asked the damsel for a drink from her pitcher, she would give him a drink and also give his camels water. (Genesis 24:15) *"And it came to pass, before He had done speaking, that, behold, Rebekah came out, who was born to Bethuel,* son *of Milcah, the wife of Nahor, Abraham's brother, with her pitcher upon her shoulder."*

When the servant's eyes saw Rebekah and how beautiful and fair she was to look at, he ran to meet her. And, as Rebekah filled her pitcher with water, up came the servant and asked for a drink of water from her pitcher. (Genesis 24:19) *"And when she had done giving him drink, she said, I will draw water for thy camels*

The Great Reunion

also, until they have done drinking."

The **Lord** answered the servant's prayer. I am sure at this time this servant thought to himself, "My Master Isaac, will surely love this beautiful woman."

After much persuasion, the family of Rebekah agreed to let her go if she wanted. She had been listening to all that the servant had been telling her father and of how the servant had prayed for the **Lord** to show him a sign by asking for a drink and watering the camels also. The servant brought forth jewels of silver and gold for Rebekah and also beautiful clothes. He gave gifts to her mother and sisters. So Rebekah, when asked if she would go with this servant to be the wife of Isaac, she answered, "I will go".

Isaac was in the field meditating when he looked up and saw the camel caravan coming. When Rebekah lifted her eyes and saw Isaac she jumped off her camel for she had asked the servant who this man was. And when the servant answered that it was Isaac, she took a vail, as was the custom in those days, and covered her face.

(Genesis 24:67) *"And Isaac brought her into his mother Sarah's tent, and took Rebekah, and she became his wife; and he loved her: and Isaac was comforted after his mother's death."*

Abraham once again took a wife and her name was Keturah. The Bible doesn't tell just how many daughters Abraham had by his wife Keturah, but it does say he had six more sons that Keturah birthed for him. They were Zimran, Jokshan, Median, Midian, Ishbak and Shuah. (Genesis 25:2).

The Bible does tell us that Abraham gave gifts unto

all his sons. Then he sent them away unto the East Country and away from the "promised son", Isaac. (Genesis 25:5) *"And Abraham gave all that he had unto Isaac."*

Abraham lived to be a hundred and seventy-five years old. Then he died and his sons, Isaac and Ishmael, buried him in the cave of Machpelah with Sarah.

Ishmael lived to an old age of one hundred thirty seven years and gave up the ghost, and Isaac lived to be one hundred eighty years old and gave up the ghost.

The Great Reunion

Chapter 7

Isaac and Rebekah had twin sons. But even in the womb of Rebekah the twins struggled together so much so that Rebekah was concerned of the feelings within her body and inquired of the **Lord** why it was so. The **Lord** told her then that there were two nations in her womb and two manner of people and that one people would be stronger than the other. (Genesis 25:23)

And when Rebekah delivered the twins, Esau was born first and would be considered the eldest son, heir to his father Isaac's blessing. But as Esau was coming out of the womb, Jacob took hold of Esau's heel.

Years later, Jacob would manipulate his brother Esau, and steal those birthright blessings from Esau his brother. And going further, still with the help of his mother Rebekah, he would also deceive his blind father Isaac and through this deception he would also receive the blessings of Isaac, which rightfully belonged to his brother Esau. At this time, there were no taking back of blessings once they were bestowed upon the receiver. Through bitter tears and with much sorrow Esau wept and said to himself, "Someday, I will kill my brother Jacob for this deception he has done."

Jacob left the presence of his family through the fear of knowing what the intentions of his brother Esau were. He went into a far land from which his mother had come. And Jacob went to be with his mother's brother and Jacob's uncle, Laban.

When he arrived in that country, the first woman he met was Laban's daughter Rachel. She was more than

The Great Reunion

fair to look at. She was beautiful and Jacob was in love with Rachel even from the beginning. He spoke to Laban and said: (Genesis 29:18) *"And Jacob loved Rachel; and said, 'I will serve thee seven years for Rachel thy younger daughter."* Now, there shouldn't have been a misunderstanding here that Jacob was talking and bargaining for only Rachel.

Laban must have thought to himself after the seven years, we will do it my way. It was the custom in those days for the oldest daughter to marry first. Laban might have thought that his oldest daughter Leah would have already been taken when he made the bargain with Jacob seven years before. Jacob, himself being the deceiver he was with Esau, should not have been surprised when he was also deceived. So when Jacob had served the seven years that he promised Laban for Rachel, he said unto him, (Genesis 29:21) *"Give me my wife, for my days are fulfilled, that I may go in unto her."*

Laban, still open as to what his own personal needs were, used trickery at the last minute, just as Jacob did to Esau. He got Jacob drunk at a feast supposedly to celebrate his coming into Laban's family as a son-in-law. (Genesis 29:23) *"And it came to pass in the evening, that he took Leah his daughter and brought her to him; and he went in unto her."*

The next morning Jacob saw what had been done unto him; and then Laban said to Jacob. (Genesis 29:26) *"It must not be done in our country, to give the younger before the first-born."*

In reality what Laban was saying to Jacob was "turn about is fair play". I'm sure when Jacob first talked to

Laban and telling him the reasons for him leaving his own home and coming to him, the matter between himself and his brother Esau must have been brought up. So now Laban was the same as saying "pay back is terrible, isn't it Jacob?"

In the meantime Jacob made another agreement with Laban, saying he would serve him another seven years for the hand of the wife he wanted from the very first. But I'm sure Jacob got a better understanding this time than he had the first seven years before.

Leah was the first to bare Jacob a son and she called his name Reuben. After this Leah conceived again and bore Jacob another son and she called his name Simeon. She conceived the third time and bore Jacob a son that she called Levi. The fourth time she conceived and bore another son and called him Judah. These were the first four sons of Jacob.

After marrying Rachel, her womb was closed up and she was unable to bare children. Rachel envied her sister and became angry with Jacob and said, (Genesis 30:3) "B*ehold my maid Bilhah, go in unto her; and she shall bear upon my knees, that I may also have children by her.*"

Would you believe that Rachel was putting Jacob into the same trap that his grandmother, Sarah, had put his grandfather Abraham in? (Genesis 30:5) *"And Bilhah conceived, and bore Jacob a son. And his name was called Dan. And Bilhah conceived again and bore Jacob another son, and his name was called Naphtoli."*

When Leah saw that she had left childbearing age, she took Zilpah, her maid, and gave her to Jacob as a wife. (Genesis 30:12) *"And Zilpah, Leah's maid, bares Jacob a son."* This made seven sons for Jacob. And Leah named the son Zilpah had bore for Jacob, and called him Gad. Zilpah conceived again and bore Jacob another son and his name was Asher. Leah wanted greatly to have another son for Jacob. And **God** heard her crying to him and she conceived again and bore Jacob his sixth son by her. She called his name Zebulun. Once again Leah conceived and bore Jacob a daughter and named her Dinah.

(Genesis 30:22) *"And **God** remembered Rachel, and **God** hearkened to her, and opened her womb."* By this time Jacob already had ten sons. Six by Leah, two by Bilhah, (Rachel's maid) and two by Zilpah, (Leah's maid). So now Rachel conceived for the first time and bore Jacob a son named Joseph.

Jacob had served Laban a total of twenty years when he left Laban and went back to his own country. On the way back to his country Jacob took his two wives, his two women servant's, and his eleven sons and daughter and passed over the ford at the Jabbok river.

(Genesis 32:24) *"And Jacob was left alone; and there wrestled a man with him until the breaking of the day."* Some say this man was an angel of the **Lord**. I personally believe it was **Christ** Himself.

(Genesis 32:27) *"At this time the man said unto him, 'What is thy name?' And he said, Jacob."* And the man said (Genesis 32:28) *"Thy name shall be called no more Jacob, but Israel: for as a prince hast thou power with **God** and with men, and hast prevailed."*

I wonder how many people realize that the country

of Israel got its name this very night that Jacob, which means deceiver, got his name changed to Israel by the man with whom he wrestled all night.

Let me ask you? Are you wrestling now with the **Lord** over something such as your own salvation (rescue from a great danger) or perhaps some personal sin you have, that only you and the **Lord** know about. I can assure you he does know about it; and right now he is saying to you: "Let me cast that sin from you."

Just as Jacob would not turn loose until he got a promise that the **Lord** would bless him, so let it be with you! So as Jacob's promise of a blessing was fulfilled, a whole nation was named after his new name Israel. You see, **God** didn't like his old name Jacob, that meant deceiver. So it may be with you, my friend. But you can believe there is something about you that **God** wants to change. All you must do is say Amen, which means, "so be it." That can happen to you right now, before you have even finished reading this book. If you are willing to make that change, I can promise you it will happen even before you finish this book.

You may say, "How can you promise such a thing?" To that I say, "I didn't promise it, but the **Holy Ghost** that lives in me and is having me to write these words, promises it. While you are reading say to your spirit, "Holy spirit of mine, take this matter up with the **Holy Ghost** of which John David speaks."

I can promise that if you hold fast and don't turn loose, and don't doubt, believing that what you say and ask for will come true with **God's** will. Be assured it will come to pass and soon. I am not just speaking of your needs, but things of your heart's desire. How do I know? Because my Bible says it is so. (John 14:14) *"If ye shall ask anything in my name, I will do it."* Now read (Mark 11:24) *"Therefore I say unto you, what things so ever ye desire, when ye pray, believe that ye receive them, and ye shall have them."*

What better proof do we need when **Jesus** made both of these statements himself? If you have not already surrendered to the blood that the **Lord** and **Savior** spilt at Calvary's Hill, from the cross on which he died, and received and accepted him as your **Lord** and **Savior**, you need to do that right now. That needs to be your first want and the desire of your heart. This then will make you eligible for all the rest. Amen.

Going back to Israel, formerly Jacob, his wife Rachel became pregnant again. At the time to give birth Rachel had such a hard labor giving birth that she died. She was buried in the way to Ephrath, which is Bethlehem.

What a sorrowful time Israel had; only the knowledge of the son that Rachel had given him at the time of her death spared some of his sorrow. Israel named him Benjamin. Benjamin would be the twelfth son that Israel had. These twelve sons would become known as the twelve tribes of Israel, and so are still today.

Chapter 8

Joseph and Benjamin were full brothers, whereas the other ten were their half brothers and the other ten were extremely jealous over Benjamin and Joseph, but more so over Joseph. Joseph would have dreams and would tell them his dreams that would indicate them bowing down to him. They were so jealous of Joseph that hatred built up against Joseph. This jealousy and hatred built to a boiling point. One day the ten brothers were watching over the flock when Joseph came by orders from his father Israel to check and see that all was well with the flocks and with the ten brothers. Upon seeing Joseph coming, the ten brothers conspired to sell Joseph to a band of renegade slavers, where he would later be resold in Egypt. From their conspiracy, many years later the people of Israel would be saved.

Joseph, because his faith never wavered, would become of high rank in the land of Egypt – second in command next to the Pharaoh. As the years went by there were severe droughts that came upon the land where Israel and his people lived. There was not enough food for Israel and his people in the land.

Israel called his ten sons together telling them that he had heard that there was much food that could be bought in Egypt. Israel was getting very old and the **Lord** had blessed him abundantly through the years. So he had much money to buy food in Egypt. So his ten sons each filled sacks with gold and silver and many gifts to buy food from the Egyptians.

All ten brothers set out to Egypt to buy food leaving

the youngest son Benjamin with Israel. Benjamin was now the favorite of Israel since the ten brothers had sold Joseph into slavery and had come back from the field and told their father that he had been attacked and killed by a wild animal; showing Israel the coat of many colors which had been soaked with lamb's blood. Israel believed that Joseph, his most favorite son, was now dead, and Israel wept bitterly and mourned over Joseph for many years. I am sure Israel was very protective of Benjamin being the youngest son and also son of his beloved Rachel.

The ten brothers arrived in Egypt and as they were going about the land inquiring about buying much food, they were sent to Joseph. Many years had passed by now and Joseph was no longer a boy and the ten brothers did not recognize him. But the spirit of Joseph recognized his ten brothers immediately. As they introduced themselves by name, it became very clear to Joseph of each one's identity. Joseph was overwhelmed and had to excuse himself and go into another part of the palace to weep without being seen or recognized by his brothers.

Most men would rejoice in their brothers' calamity and would say, "OK, it's pay back time." But Joseph did not. The **Lord** had put a humble heart in him to do them no harm. However, Joseph did have a little fun with their emotions.

Joseph remembered his dreams of them when a boy and spoke roughly to them, accusing them of being spies coming into the land.

They answered in (Genesis 42:13) *"Thy servants are twelve brethren, the sons of one man in the land of*

Canaan; and, behold, the youngest is this day with our father, and one is not." When the brothers spoke of their family, Joseph carried it further and said, "That's it! You are spies."

Then to prove themselves Joseph asked that all but one be retained in prison and send that one back to their father to bring the youngest brother, Benjamin back (Genesis 42:17) *"And he put them all together into ward three days."*

On the third day Joseph said to them, "If ye be true men, leave one of your brothers in prison and take the food back to your family and bring your youngest brother back to me so that your words can be verified."

When the nine brothers returned to their father Israel and opened their sacks, they found that, their money was returned and in every brother's sack, and they were sore afraid as was Israel. Then Reuben approached his father to tell him that they had left Simeon in Egypt and were instructed to return with Benjamin. It was hard for Reuben to convince Israel to let Benjamin go back with him. (Genesis 42:37) *"And Reuben spake unto his father, saying, 'Slay my two sons, if I bring him not to thee: deliver him unto my hand, and I will bring him to thee again."*

Then the nine brothers returned to Egypt with Benjamin and double the payment for the grain, the portion that was returned to them in their sacks as they thought was an oversight, and more payment for more corn. And when they arrived in Egypt and took Benjamin before Joseph, Joseph said to the ruler, "Stay and make ready for these men to dine with me tonight." The brothers

The Great Reunion

were afraid.

And they came to the steward of Joseph's house and told him all about the money being returned in their sacks and that they had brought it again in their hand with more to pay for more food. When Joseph came home, they brought him the present that was in their hands and bowed down to him. Joseph inquired of his father and when Joseph's eyes fell upon Benjamin he went into his chambers and wept again.

Then Joseph revealed himself to his eleven brothers. (Genesis 45: 3-5) *"And Joseph said unto his brethren, 'I am Joseph; doth my father yet live?' And his brethren could not answer him; for they were troubled at his presence."*

And Joseph said unto his brethren, Come near to me, I pray you. And they came near. And he said I am Joseph your brother, whom ye sold into Egypt. Now therefore, be not grieved, nor angry with yourselves, that ye sold me hither: for **God** did send me before you to preserve life."

After Joseph had revealed himself, he said to them go and get your father and all his household, and Pharaoh has said, (Genesis 45:18) *"And take your father and your households, and come unto me: and I will give you the good of the land of Egypt, and ye shall eat the fat of the land."*

Those brothers left and went back to the land of Canaan to get their father and all of his and their households. Now the truth had to come out. Now those ten brothers had to confess to their father their evil deed of selling Joseph unto slavery. But they also told him that over the years Joseph had found favor with the Pharaoh and was appointed Governor over all of the land of Egypt.

God came to Israel in the night in a vision (Genesis 46:3) *"And he said, 'I am* **God***, the* **God** *of thy father: fear not to go down into Egypt; for I will there make of thee a great nation."*

The number whom Israel brought with him was about one hundred souls from the land of Canaan. They settled in the land of Goshen. Then Israel sent Judah before him to bring Joseph unto him and Joseph went to see his father, Israel. When seeing his father Joseph fell upon his neck and they both wept. And Israel said to Joseph, "Now I can die in peace knowing you are yet alive."

Israel was one hundred and thirty years old when he came unto Egypt, and he lived there for seventeen years and gave up the ghost, dying at the age of one hundred and forty seven.

The Great Reunion

Chapter 9

After Israel's death his brothers feared Joseph saying to each other, "Will Joseph now have his revenge for the evil we did to him?" But here was Joseph's answer to them: (Genesis 50:19-20) *"And Joseph said unto them, 'Fear not: for am I in the place of **God**?"* Now read in Genesis 50:20 where Joseph said, *"But as for you, ye thought evil against me; but **God** meant it unto good, to being to pass, as it is this day, to save much people alive."*

And Joseph remained kind and gentle to all his brothers and they all lived a very peaceable life, and the children of Israel made an oath to Joseph to take his bones up out of Egypt and bury them with his fathers Abraham, Isaac and Jacob. Joseph lived to be a hundred and ten years old and gave up the ghost.

This is the conclusion of Genesis, which I like to think of as the beginning of **God's** secrets as well as showing the perfect love **God** had for us as men. Why that much love? No man knows, only the three **Godheads** the **Father**, the **Son**, and the **Holy Ghost**. Why should we doubt this? We shouldn't. Later in this book you will see **God** proving the love about which I speak. Amen.

The Great Reunion

Chapter 10

There was a man named Moses, a man who was born of a Hebrew woman that was the wife of a man from the house of Levi. This man being from the house of Levi was probably a Godly man. At this time there was a new Pharoah who had become king over all the lands of Egypt. This Pharoah had noticed, when looking over the land of Egypt, that the Hebrew children were many in number.

Therefore, this wicked Pharoah spoke to the two midwives, Shiphrah and Puah, who usually delivered the Hebrew babies. He told them when they delivered a baby and if it was a son, they were to kill it. If it was a girl, they were to spare it and let it live.

So at the time Moses was born, his mother gave free birth, meaning she had no help. So no one knew when Moses was born, except his mother and his big sister who was eight years old. The earthly father of Moses had died after Moses was conceived in his mother's womb and so his mother was a widow. She later would tell Moses that his older brother of two years was also with her and his sister at his birth, making a total of three present at his birth.

When Moses was three months old, his mother became fearful that word would get out that she was hiding a baby. The King's command had gone out six months earlier to kill all of the Hebrew sons from that day forward. So the mother of Moses made an Ark of bulrushes – river straw – and daubed it with slime and with pitch and set Moses in the basket afloat in the river

The Great Reunion

saying, "**God** have your way." And **God** did have his way. This baby would become known as the son of Pharaoh's own daughter because she claimed him as her own son. As Moses grew into manhood he reaped the rewards of royalty, such as having great teachers of education and much worldly wealth.

Moses later found out that he was born of a Hebrew woman at birth and became thought of as a hero to the Hebrew children when one day he spied on an Egyptian smiting a Hebrew, one of his brethren. Moses slew the Egyptian that day and hid the body in the sand, but Moses deed was revealed (Exodus 2:15).

When Pharoah heard this thing, he sought to slay Moses. But Moses fled from the face of Pharoah, and dwelt in the land of Midian. The priest of Midian had seven daughters and Moses took, Zipporah, one of the daughters to wife. Zipporah bore him a son, which he called Gershom. Moses was forty years old at this time and kept the flock of Jethro, his father-in-law, who was the Midian priest.

As Moses was tending the flock that he led to the backside of the desert, he came upon a mountain called Horeb. He had intentions of grazing the flock there.

(Exodus 3:2) *"And the angel of the **Lord** appeared unto him in a flame of fire out of the midst of a bush; and he looked and behold the bush burned with fire, and the bush was not consumed."* Use your imagination to see what Moses saw! Can you imagine what Moses must have thought?

As Moses walked closer to the bush to see what was going on, the bush was burning as a wick in a lamp and still it was not being burnt up and consumed by fire. As Moses drew closer to the bush **God** called out to him (Exodus 3:5) *"Draw not nigh hither: put off they shoes from off thy feet, for the place whereon thou standest is holy ground."*

Moses was standing in **God**'s glory, on holy ground. (Exodus 3:6) *"Moreover he said, 'I am the **God** of thy father, the **God** of Abraham, the **God** of Isaac, and the **God** of Jacob. And Moses hid his face; for he was afraid to look upon **God**. "*

What an awesome thing this was for Moses! The **God** who created the heavens and the earth was taking time to talk with one man, one on one. **God** did have a plan.

He wanted to have a "Reunion" with his children, and he wanted to have that "Reunion" in the land of Canaan, the land he had given to their forefathers four hundred years before. Moses was in that plan of **God**'s to bring his children home; back to the land of Canaan, the land of milk and honey.

From the very first Moses began to argue against **God** saying many things to be in disagreement with **God**. But when **God** asked Moses, "What is that in your hand?" and Moses answered, "It's a rod." Then **God** said, "Throw it down on the ground."

The very minute Moses threw the rod down, it hit the ground as a serpent. That did shake Moses up and it got his attention. He had no doubt now that he was standing in the presence of the **Almighty** who created everything. Now Moses would listen and do as **God** commanded.

Moses was as any man would be, asking and not

understanding how and why was the **God** of the Creation wanting to use him to go bring the Hebrew children out of Egypt. (Exodus 3:20) *"And then **God** said, I will stretch out my hand, and smite Egypt with all my wonders which I will do in the midst thereof: and after that he will let you go."* **God** had spoken and now it would surely come to pass as He had said.

Just as man will do, poor Moses kept trying to give **God** a reason not to send him. (Exodus 4:13-14) *"And he said, 'O my **Lord** send, I pray thee, by the hand of him whom thou wilt send. And the anger of the **Lord** was kindled against Moses, and He said, Is not Aaron the Levite thy brother? I know that he can speak well. And also, behold, he cometh forth to meet thee: and when he seeth thee, he will be glad in his heart."*

(Exodus 4:27) *"And the **Lord** said to Aaron, 'Go into the wilderness to meet Moses'. And he went, and met him, in the mount of **God**. And kissed him."*

God was now putting these two brothers together in a reunion after forty years apart. What a brotherly joy that must have been. Moses and Aaron his brother probably visited with each other for a couple of days with Moses telling Aaron all that **God** had said to him and commanded for him to do. Aaron must have told Moses, "I knew something was up when the **Lord** spoke to me telling me to go unto you, Moses." So here two brothers, both servants of the **Lord**, were now in agreement unto one accord to go and do as **God** had commanded. So they obeyed **God** and went.

Moses and Aaron left for the land of the Pharaoh. Were they still in doubt as they were before? Not in the least, as they had by now come into one accord that **God** Himself was now leading them. And all that He had said would come to pass. But from the very beginning, when Moses and Aaron began to speak to Pharaoh telling him the **Lord God** of Israel has sent us to tell you King, "let my children of the Hebrews go", the Pharaoh's answer was "I don't know your **God**. No, what you have asked I will not do."

Through many signs and wonders **God** did unto Pharaoh, **God** was constantly telling his Hebrew children, "See, I am the **Lord** and I will bring you out from under the bondage of the Egyptians." As the **Lord** told Moses to smite the waters of Egypt with the rod of his hand, all the waters including the rivers, lakes and wells turned into blood and were such for seven days.

Each time that Moses wanted **God** to do something; the Bible says he would cry unto the **Lord,** always in a question. Why this or why that? And always crying to the **Lord**, the **Lord** would do what he asked. The Hebrew children were always murmuring, complaining to Moses, and as usual, Moses would go to **God** crying for help.

Moses and Aaron brought a warning to the Pharaoh that unless he let the Hebrew children go to the **Lord** and worship him, all the first born in the land of Egypt shall die. (Exodus 11:5) *"And all the firstborn in the land of Egypt shall die, from the firstborn of Pharaoh that siteth upon his throne, even unto the first born of the maid-servant that is behind the mill: and all the firstborn of beasts."*

At this time the **Lord** spoke to Moses and Aaron and told them to tell the Hebrew people to take a lamb without

The Great Reunion

spot or blemish and kill it and put the blood over the door posts of the Hebrew children's houses; then I will pass over the Hebrew children, and this shall come to be known to all as the **Lord's** Passover. Until this day, this night that the **Lord** saw the blood of the lamb on the doorposts is still remembered and celebrated by the Hebrew children.

After this awesome night of death and fear, the Pharaoh who's own son died, came even in the night unto Moses and Aaron and said to them, "Take everything of the Hebrew children and go and leave this land of Egypt now." So the children of the Hebrews got all of their possessions together and started on their journey, leaving Egypt and traveling toward Canaan, the promised land of milk and honey. There were about six hundred thousand men, besides the women and children. **God** was having them come out of Egypt to His "Reunion" in Canaan land.

But afterwards the Pharaoh's people realized that the Hebrew children had left Egypt, and they began to say unto Pharaoh, "Whom will now serve us?" And Pharaoh got his soldiers together and they mounted six hundred chosen chariots, the best they had, and many foot soldiers and pursued the children of Israel.

When the children of Israel lifted up their eyes and saw the army of Pharaoh marching after them, fear came upon them and they began to cry out unto the **Lord** and unto Moses saying, "Did we not have enough graves in Egypt? That you have brought us out here to die?" Then Moses cried out again unto the **Lord** saying, "**Lord**, the mountains are on our left side and also on our right side,

A Road That Won't Travel

and the army of Pharaoh is behind us, and we face the sea before us. What do we do now?"

I believe the **Lord** maybe scolded Moses at this time, telling him, "Moses, why do you always cry out to me? I have already told you and proved myself to you. You have the power you need in your right hand by the rod, which is my token to you."

In Exodus 14:16, **God** said, *"Stop crying to me, but lift up the rod, and stretch out thine hand over the sea and divide it: and the children of Israel shall go on dry land through the midst of the sea"* **God** told Moses from the very beginning his rod would be a token of his great power. All he had to do was use it with faith, believing, and all the mountains of his troubles would cease to be. Moses, like many of **God's** children today, kept forgetting.

My Dear Friend, I am sure you have right now some small hills that are in front of you, if not mountains. But I have good news for you. You only need to lift that rod (your Bible) you do have, up as Moses did lift his rod. In the Bible, we have just as strong of a rod as Moses had. We have the continuous word of **God Almighty** right now in our hand. **God's** word says it. I do believe that it settles it. Now by faith, stand firm against the mountain of trouble. **God** will do it. Why? Because He is love, faithful to His word, full of truth and mercy. If we will receive and accept His Son **Jesus**, we are His, adopted by the death and resurrection of His dear Son, with the adoption signed in His BLOOD. Amen.

Yes, they did cross the Red Sea on dry ground. I believe they did this because my Bible says it did happen.

My Bible, **God's** Holy Word, also says that when the

army of Pharaoh followed the exact trail that the Hebrew children had taken, the waters came back together as they were before and swallowed up the army of Pharaoh and all died.

God, many times had proven Himself to the children of Israel by showing great wonders and saying, "I am with you. Still." (Exodus 16:2) *"And the whole congregation of the children of Israel murmured against Moses and Aaron in the wilderness."*

They complained of no meat, no bread, no water and all the time they were full. So really what they were saying was, we want tomorrow's groceries today. Had they stood fast in praying and worshipping and giving **God** "thank you", the long journey of forty years could have been made in six months maximum. And that would have been dragging their feet.

God sent meat by the way of a blowing wind that brought quail and manna. You may ask, "How long did **God** send this unto His children of Israel?" My answer to that would be, as a man would say, "As long as my children needs meat, I will provide until it runs out." But with our **God** that never happens. (Exodus 16:35) *"And the children of Israel did eat manna forty years, until they came to a land inhabited; they did eat manna, until they came unto the borders of the land of Canaan."*

During these forty years of the children of Israel wandering in the wilderness, **God** made a new covenant with His people giving Moses the Ten Commandments – **God's** laws they were to keep. These Ten Commandments became known as "The Law". They are commanded today to be kept by all of **God's** children.

Chapter 11

The **Ten Commandments**, given to and written by Moses about thirty-five hundred years ago, are still to be kept today as far as **God** is now concerned.

This would still be known as "**The Law**" even today.

1. Thou shalt have no other god's before me.

2. Thou shalt not make unto thee any graven image, or any likeness of anything that is in heaven above, or that is in the earth beneath, or that is in the water under the earth.

3. Thou shalt not take the name of the Lord thy God in vain; for the Lord will not hold him guiltless that taketh his name in vain.

4. Remember the Sabbath Day, to keep it holy.

5. Honor thy father and thy mother: that thy days may be long upon the land which the Lord thy God giveth thee.

6. Thou shalt not kill.

7. Thou shalt not commit adultery.

8. Thou shalt not steal.

9. Thou shalt not bear false witness against thy neighbor.

10. Thou shalt not covet thy neighbors house, thou shalt not covet thy neighbor's wife, nor his manservant, nor his maidservant, not his ox, nor his ass, nor any thing that is thy neighbor's.

The Great Reunion

During this time **God** gave instructions to Moses concerning the building of the Ark, of the Testimony, the Tabernacle, and all of the furnishings that went into the Ark.

The **Lord** had Moses, during these forty years of being in the wilderness, to write the first five books of the Holy Scriptures Genesis, Exodus, Leviticus, Numbers and Deuteronomy. These first five books would become known as **God's** Holy Word the Bible of that time.

God would not allow Moses to go into the promised land of Canaan. So Moses died at the age of one hundred and twenty years. (Deut. 34:6-7) *"And He (**God**) buried him in a valley in the land of Moab, over against Beth-pear; but no man knoweth of his sepulcher unto this day. And Moses was a hundred and twenty years old when he died; his eye was not dim, nor his natural force abated."* For some reason, **God** hid Moses body; only **God** knows where.

After the death of Moses, Joshua became heir to Moses' leadership. Joshua was the one who took the children of Israel across the Jordan into the land of Canaan. He led them in all of their wars and was responsible for the issuance of all the spoils of the enemy, including the dividing of the land.

All this time **God** was with the children of Israel and they were victorious, having victory after victory against their enemies. **God** was with Joshua. (Joshua 24:29) *"And it came to pass after these things, that Joshua the son of Nun, the servant of the **Lord**, died being a hundred and ten."*

Chapter 12

The next person who came to the light of being a leader of **God's** people was a man named Samuel. Samuel was a judge at first, and later on he was a prophet, a man of **God**.

Samuel was, almost from the beginning, vowed from his mother, Hannah, to be a gift unto the **Lord**. (I Samuel 1:11) *"And she vowed a vow, and said, 'O **Lord** of hosts, if thou wilt indeed look on the affliction of thine handmaid, and remember me, and not forget thine handmaid, but wilt give unto thine handmaid a man child, then I will give him unto the **Lord** all the days of his life, and there shall no razor come upon his head."*

Hannah was barren and she was getting up in years of age. So after she went many years unable to conceive, she made *the Lord* a deal. If you will give him to me, then at the age of three, I'll give him to you.

I must say it was a hard deal for Hannah to keep, but she did keep it; at the age of three Samuel was brought to Eli, the priest, and Hannah told Eli of the vow she had made unto the **Lord** concerning Samuel. And Eli took the child Samuel into the house of the **Lord** that day.

I can only think at the time Hannah made this vow unto the **Lord**, that Elkanah, her husband, must have been told of the vow his wife made unto the **Lord**. Elkanah must have also been in agreement with Hannah that if the **Lord** allowed Hannah to conceive after all of these years he would allow the child to be given to the **Lord** at the age of three.

The time came for Hannah and her husband Elkanah

to stand behind that vow that they made unto the **Lord** when the child became three years of age. I can only imagine the tears that were spilled by these parents when they said goodbye to their little three-year-old child and left him with Eli, the priest, in the House of the **Lord**. I'm sure the **Lord** prepared the heart of the three year old for the separation. For a normal child, who has had much love from his family, would have been terribly upset to be left by his parents.

(I Samuel 3:1) *"And the child Samuel ministered unto the **Lord** before Eli, and the word of the **Lord** was precious in those days; there was no open vision."*

(I Samuel 3:19-20) *"And Samuel grew and the **Lord** was with him, and did let none of his words fall to the ground. And all of Israel from Dan even to Beersheba knew that Samuel had been established to be a prophet of the **Lord**."*

The children of Israel murmured to Samuel the prophet, saying, "All the nations around us have a king, give us one." After much murmuring the **Lord** told Samuel to anoint them a king.

The **Lord** revealed to Samuel to anoint Saul, the son of Kish, as king over all the people of Israel. And Saul reined for forty years over the people of Israel and in war the Philistines slew Saul's three sons, Jonathan, Abinadab and Melchi-shua and wounded even Saul so that he fell backward upon his sword and died.

Afterwards the **Lord** spoke to Samuel and said, go unto the house of Jessie and anoint David, son of Jessie, who killed Goliath the Philistine giant, and make him king over the children of Israel. (II Samuel 5:4) *"David was* *thirty years old when he began to reign, and he reigned forty years."*

David the king was a righteous man and a good king. But as human nature would have it, David had a weakness for women. (II Samuel 11:2) *"It came to pass in an evening tide, that David arose from off his bed, and walked upon the roof of the kings house: and from the roof he saw a woman washing herself; and the woman was very beautiful to look upon."*

David sent for this woman knowing she was the wife of Uriah the Hittite, one of his most loyal soldiers. David knowingly committed adultery, against **God's** law. Still he said to himself, "I want her and I will have her." King David went against **God's** Commandments. "Thou shalt not commit adultery." He lay with Bathsheba, Uriah's wife. (II Samuel 11:5) *"And the woman conceived, and sent and told King David, 'I am with child'."*

What a terrible thing. Today's philosophy would be, "So what. Get an abortion". But even thirty five hundred years ago, people knew that at the time of conception there was a live baby with a spirit and a soul within the body of the woman. So to rid King David of this sin of adultery he sent for his servant soldier Uriah. David's intention was to have Uriah come home to Bathsheba and have him sleep with Bathsheba. Then he could hide his sin by making it look like Uriah impregnated his own wife, Bathsheba. David and Bathsheba both were in full agreement to do this sin of deceit. David just kept getting himself into deeper sin as he tried to cover up his sin of adultery.

Uriah the Hittite soon arrived at the king's house. But

with the loyalty Uriah had toward his men whom he left sleeping on the battlefield, he would not go to his own house and sleep with his wife, Bathsheba. Even with the king's coaching Uriah still would not enjoy the comfort of his bed and the comfort of his wife. Instead he slept outside with the other servants. **If only King** David had been this loyal to Uriah this cover up would have never been necessary. "If only."

In fear of his sin of adultery catching up with him, David was now willing to go unto any length to keep his sin a secret. So he wrote Joab, the commanding General of his front line army a letter and he sealed it and had Uriah the Hittite carry the letter to Joah on his return to the front lines. So Uriah carried the message of his own execution for the murder that David and Joab were about to commit. (II Samuel 11:15) *"And he* (David) *wrote in the letter saying. 'Set ye Uriah in the forefront of the hottest battle and retire ye* (pull back) *from him, that he may be smitten,* (killed) *and die."*

One sin led to another and those sins of King David just kept snow balling until **God** said, "Enough!" So the **Lord** sent Nathan, the prophet, unto King David and Nathan chastised the King with a parable saying, "Once there was a rich man who had many lambs and his flock was to over flowing and there was a poor man who had only one ewe lamb and this poor man loved this little eye with all of his heart. Then one day the rich man saw the poor man's little ewe and wanted it. So he sent his servants to steal the ewe. The rich man did kill and eat the poor man's ewe. King David went into a rage before Nathan the prophet. (II Samuel 12:5) *"And David's anger* *was greatly kindled against the man; and he said to Nathan, 'As the **Lord** liveth, the man that has done this thing shall surely die."*

I'm sure at this time Nathan the prophet must have said to King David, "Are you sure the penalty of this sin should be death?" I am equally as sure that the King's answer was "Yes." Then Nathan replied, (II Samuel 12:7) *"Thou art the man, thus sayeth the **Lord God** of Israel. I did anoint thee king over Israel, and I delivered thee out of the hand of Saul.*

I can see as David would say to Nathan, "I rescind that penalty of which I spoke." But **God,** even in his mercy, would himself pronounce a penalty on David's sin. The child that Bathsheba bore unto David would die. It lived long enough to become David's favorite out of twelve sons he had. David wept and grieved over the loss of this son. (II Samuel 23:2-3) *"The Spirit of the **Lord** spake by me, and his word was in my tongue. The **God** of Israel said, 'The rock of Israel spake to me, He that ruleth over men must be just, ruling in the fear of **God**."* **God** had pleaded with David and still David did not hearken to His voice.

(Act 13:22) *"And when He had removed him, He raised up unto them David to be their King; to whom also He gave testimony, and said, 'I have found David the son of Jessie, a man after mine own heart, which shall fulfill all my will."* **God** loved David dearly, but **God** loved him no more than He loves you and me.

King David had much heartbreak through his forty years of reign as King over Israel. Amnon raped his sister Tamar. Absalom, Ammon's older brother, murdered

The Great Reunion

Amnon for the rape of their sister. Later Absalom joined in a conspiracy to overthrow his own father, King David, from the throne. In the revolt Absalom himself died by hanging. While riding his horse, his long, beautiful, red hair caught in the bough of a tree and hung him.

David mourned greatly with grief for his son Absalom saying, (II Samuel 18: 33) *"Oh my son Absalom, my son, my son Absalom! Would **God** I had died for thee, O Absalom, my son, my son!"*

Every way David turned there was always the troublesome spirit in front of him. Even as he lay in his bed sore from old age and sickness, there was always word coming to him of a plot to usurp the throne. Another one of his sons named Adonijah plotted to overthrow David's throne. But David was not a king easily defeated. Adonijah was the brother of Absalom. Their mother was Haggith. But King David had another son named Solomon by Bath-sheba. Adonijah was reigning on David's throne and David was not aware of it being old and sick. But Nathan the prophet came to Beth-sheba the mother of Solomon saying, (I Kings 1:11) *"Hast thou not heard that Adonijah the son of Haggith doth reign, and David our lord knoweth it not?"*

Nathan also told Beth-sheba in I Kings 1:13: *"Go and get thee in unto King David, and say unto him, 'Didst not thou, my lord, O King, swear unto this handmaid,' saying, 'Assuredly Solomon thy son shall reign after me, and he shall sit upon my throne? Why then doth Adonijah reign?"* David brought his son Solomon into the inheritance of his kingship and set him upon the throne.

Chapter 13

When Solomon took the throne he felt inadequate and unsure of himself to lead **God's** children, the Israelites. So he prayed to the **Lord God** of Israel to give him great wisdom that would allow him to lead the children of Israel in a **Godly** and obedient way of living unto the Holy One of Israel. Because Solomon did not ask for great wealth, glory and honor for himself, **God** gave him the wisdom he asked for. And the wisdom given to him by **God** also caused him to become the wealthiest King on earth. Solomon still holds that record even until today.

King David was told, by **God** that he had too much blood on his hands to build a temple for **God**. David had wanted to build a temple for **God** to live in and among his children that would bring glory to **God**. But **God** told David that David's son Solomon would be allowed to build the temple.

In those days, (I Kings 3:2) *"only the people sacrificed in high places, because there was no house built unto the name of the **Lord**."* This is why David was so concerned about building a temple for **God**.

King Solomon also wrote some of the Psalms that are written in the book of Psalms; he wrote Proverbs while in search of the wisdom which he was asking of **God**. He wrote again in Ecclesiastes about life as **God** had intended for it to be. Even from the start of **God's** creation of man, the twelve chapters of Ecclesiastes tell men and women and also children how to deal with their life's problems.

The Great Reunion

Solomon also wrote a book named "Song of Solomon". This is one of the greatest love stories ever told by any writer or author of any book ever written, including "Gone with the Wind". The Song of Solomon was written about nine hundred and seventy years before the coming of **Christ**.

Chapter 14

I do believe if every person, young or old, who intends to join in holy marriage would both read this book together, one chapter at a time and discuss it in its entirety, they would know 'yes' or 'no' if they can be in one accord with each other as **Jesus** said. (Matthew 19:6) *"Wherefore they are no more twain, but one flesh. What therefore **God** hath joined together, let not man put asunder."* I believe the divorce rate would be cut in half.

Think about this great wisdom, this great knowledge, this great understanding that is now, this very day, open to all of **God's** children. Why? Not only does **God** love us just as much as He did Solomon the King, but we have our own master who is standing by **God's** right hand and who is willing to go to bat for us.

The Great Reunion

Chapter 15

The interest of my thoughts of other kings of the children of Israel brings to my mind one King Hezekiah. (II Kings 18:2) *"Twenty and five years old was he when he began to reign; and he reigned twenty and nine years in Jerusalem."*

(II Kings 18:5) *"He trusted in the **Lord God** of Israel; so that after him was none like him among all the kings of Judah, nor any that were before him."*

One of the main events during the reign of King Hezekiah was what happened to the King of Assyria when he came forth against the small band of Hekekiah's soldiers. Sennacherib, the King of Assyria knew that he had the army of Hezekiah outnumbered by thirty-to-one. So he sent messengers to King Hezekiah saying, "Give unto me all your wealth, all your young people to be my servants and the servants of my people." Hezekiah went to the **Lord** in prayer praying, "**Lord**, help me."

The **Lord** sent his one angel who was dressed for battle. (II Kings 19:35) *"And it came to pass that night, that the angel of the **Lord** sent out and smote in the camp of the Assyrians an hundred fourscore and five thousand* (185,000) *and when they arose early in the morning, behold, they were all dead corpses.*

Think of this. One angel in one night killed 185,000. I want you to keep this in your mind because later in this book, I will be telling you of the power of more angels. So remember this one angel.

Right after this, the King of Assyria, Sennacherib, tucked his tail between his legs and went back down that same road of which he had come. It came to pass after he was back at his house in Nineveh worshipping his god, Nisrock, that Adrammeleck and Sharezar his own sons killed him with a sword.

As the old saying would go, like father, like son. (II Kings 20:1) *"In those days was Hezekiah sick unto death. And the prophet Isaiah the son of Amoz came to him, and said unto him, 'Thus saith the **Lord**, Set thine house in order; for thou shalt die, and not live."*

Now here was King Hezekiah in the prime of his life not even forty years old, and Isaiah the prophet was telling him, "King. get ready for you will be dying very shortly." No wonder Hezekiah turned his face to the wall and wept sorely with bitter tears. I believe Hezekiah must have said to the **Lord**, "What was this that you promised King David? That someone would reign of his seed upon the throne as King forever." Then he would probably say to the **Lord**, "**Lord** I have no son. So how can his seed reign if I die?"

As Isaiah was leaving the King and walked through the court yard, the word of the **Lord** came to him, saying, (II Kings 20:5-6) *"Turn again, and tell Hezekiah the captain of my people, Thus saith the **Lord**, The **God** of David thy father, I have heard thy prayer, I have seen thy tears; behold, I will heal thee: on the third day thou shalt go up unto the house of the **Lord**. And I will add unto thy days, fifteen years."*

What a mighty **God** we serve. He just says it and it is done. We still have that power of asking, and it will be done and even more in this day if we ask in the name of **Jesus**. Remember he is at the right hand side of **God** the **Father**. I will tell you much more later about this same man **Jesus** who stands by **God's** right hand.

During the first three years after **God** granted Hezekiah an additional fifteen years, a son was born to Hezekiah. He was named Manasseh, who was the only son Hezekiah had. After fifteen years Hezekiah died and was buried with his fathers.

Hezekiah's son Manasseh was twelve years old at the time of his father's death and began his reign at that age. He reigned for fifty-five years as King in Jerusalem.

During this time, the record of the Bible tells us Manasseh was one of the most wicked of all the Kings to this time. (II Chronicles 33:6) *"And he caused his children to pass through the fire (*sacrificed his own children) *in the valley of the son of Hinnom: also he observed times, and used witchcraft, and dealth with a familiar spirit, and with wizards; he wrought much evil in the sight of the* **Lord***, to provoke Him to anger."*

In the end Manasseh repented to the **Lord God** of Israel. But he caused much heartbreak for his people before he repented. Manasseh died at the age of sixty-seven and was buried with his fathers.

Manasseh had a son named Amon who was twenty-two years old when he started his reign. Amon started his reign being very wicked as his father started out. His own servant conspired against him, slaying him in his own house. Amon never humbled himself to the **Lord** before his death.

The Great Reunion

Chapter 16

Tradition has suggested that Ezra wrote both 1st and 2nd Chronicles, getting his information from the books of Samuel and Kings. Both Chronicles were written four hundred to four hundred and fifty years before **Christ**.

Before I leave the books of the Old Testament, which I believe were written for the sole purpose of bringing men to see how **God** the **Father**, the **Son**, and the **Holy Ghost** were preparing all **God's** children to watch and be ready for the very coming of the Messiah, who is called the **Christ**.

I want to install within this book some of the scriptures that speak of that **Christ**. In the very beginning of Genesis, **God** Himself was speaking of this very **Christ**. (Genesis 3:15) *"And I will put enmity between thee and the woman, and between thy seed and her seed; it shall bruise they head, and thou shalt bruise his heel.*

All through the thirty-nine books of the Old Testament, the writers would write of the coming of the **Christ**. One of the other scriptures that were written about the things that would be done to the **Christ** is found in Isaiah 53:4: *"Surely He had borne our griefs, and carried our sorrows; yet we did esteem Him.* (Didn't recognize him) *He was stricken, smitten of* **God**, *and afflicted."*

Then Isaiah wrote *"but He was wounded for our transgressions,* (willful sinning) *and He was bruised for our iniquities*; (lawlessness) *the chastisement of our peace was upon Him; and with His stripes we are healed."* Amen. With those holy stripes we are all healed.

The Great Reunion

Had there, not been healing in those stripes, then Christ would not have had them put on him. It was his choice to have them.

In Isaiah 53:12): *"Therefore will I divide Him a portion with the great, and He shall divide the spoil with the strong; because He hath poured out His soul unto death; and He was numbered with the transgressors; and He bare the sin of many, and made intercession for the transgressors."* Speaking of **Christ**, so many times **God** would look for His children and would always be merciful; wanting to have that "Reunion" once again with them.

I do feel led to bring the scriptures of the book of Malachi, which was written by Malachi. To begin, I want to point out (Malachi 3:1) *"Behold, I will send my messenger, and he shall prepare the way before me: and the **Lord**, whom ye seek, shall suddenly come to His temple, even the messenger of the covenant, whom ye delight in; behold, he shall come saith the **Lord**."*

This scripture is speaking of John the Baptist being the forerunner of **Christ**. He was the voice spoken of in the New Testament. (John 1:34) *"And I saw and bare record that this is the **Son of God**."*

Also Malachi wrote the best known verse in his book, which is (Malachi 3:6) *"For I am the **Lord**, I change not; therefore ye sons of Jacob are not consumed."*

What **God** is saying in this verse is: "If I were a changing **God** in mind or in thought, the human race would be completely consumed because of our wicked deeds. But our **Heavenly Father** is so merciful, full of love, and so graceful, that He still wanted to have this

"Reunion" with us that this book speaks about.

All thirty-nine books of the Old Testament are saying: He is coming, be ready, and expect Him. These thirty-nine books are all saying the same thing that the enmity **God** spoke of in the first book of the Bible (Genesis 3:15) is on its way. Watch and be ready. His "Reunion" is now coming and is on its way. Amen.

The Great Reunion

Part 2

The New Testament - The Blood Covenant

Matthew, Mark, Luke, and John, the Four Gospels

The Great Reunion

Chapter 1

Matthew, one of **Jesus'** disciples, is the author of this Gospel. It was written about the sixty years after the death of **Jesus**. The book begins with a genealogy of **Christ** through His legal, though not natural father, Joseph.

Following a brief description of **Jesus'** birth and His childhood, Matthew tells of the baptism of **Jesus** by John the Baptist so the scriptures of the Bible might be fulfilled. Matthew also writes about the ministry of **Jesus** beginning with chapter five going right through chapter twenty-eight.

The birth of our **Lord** and **Savior** is the most marvelous miracle of all historical times. Of all creations, from the beginning **Jesus** was the very best thing that has ever come to men and women.

(Matthew 1:18) *"Now the birth of **Jesus Christ** was on this wise: when as His mother Mary was espoused to Joseph, before they came together, she was found with child of the **Holy Ghost**."*

The Holy Virgin would become mother to the **Savior** of all men and women; the Salvation that all men and women had looked for. (Rescue from great danger)

Even from the very first, Satan was out to kill this child, for he knew who He was. He knew the purpose of His birth was to bring all men and women into "The Great Reunion" He was going to have with His children. **God Almighty's** "Great Reunion" was coming to pass.

(Matthew 2:1) *"Now when **Jesus** was born in Bethlehem of Judea in the days of Herod the King,* behold, there came wise men from the east to Jerusalem." These wise men had seen a star. And the angel of the **Lord** had told these wise men to go worship the one under the star, a babe in a manager who was to sit on the throne as King for all eternity.

This troubled Herod the King. His first thought was "no one will take my kingship." So he told the wise men, "When you find Him bring me word that I may come and worship Him also." This is a lie from the king.

Herod the King evidently thought he was smarter than these wise men. (Matthew 2:12) *"And being warned of* **God** *in a dream that they should not return to Herod, they departed into their own country another way."*

It's amazing just to think about it. These wise men must have all had the same dream this night, for they were all in one accord believing that they should take another way home, probably the long way, to bypass going unto Herod the King.

(Matthew 2:16) *"Then Herod when he saw that he was mocked of the wise men, was exceeding wroth and sent forth* (his army) *and slew all the children that were in Bethlehem and in all the coasts thereof, from two years and under, according to the time which he had diligently enquired of the wise men."*

Use your imagination; there were no babies under two years old left in that town or even the whole coastline. None! No wonder the prophet Jeremiah wrote in the Old Testament these words. (Jeremiah 31:15) *"Thus saith the* **Lord***; A voice was heard in Ramah, lamentation, and bitter weeping; Rahel weeping for her children refused to be comforted for her children, because they* *were not.*" I can only think this King Herod must even today be in eternal hell. (The lake of fire).

Yes, Joseph was the father assigned to be the watchman of **Jesus** and his wife, Mary. Both would have to be constantly careful to be on the alert for the things of Satan that would be coming against **Jesus**.

Through the next few years **Jesus** must have kept constant study of the scriptures. When He was twelve years old, Mary and Joseph had gone to Jerusalem as they did every year for the feast of the Passover and on their way back home they had traveled three days and discovered that **Jesus** wasn't with them. They turned back to Jerusalem and when they arrived they found Him in the temple sitting in the midst of the religious teachers, both hearing them and asking them questions. And all that heard Him, as well as His mother and Joseph, were astonished concerning His knowledge and understanding of questions and answers

When His mother, Mary, asked **Jesus** why He had tarried behind and not kept up with the company they were traveling with, **Jesus** answered. (Luke 2:49) "*How is it that ye sought me? Wist ye not that I must be about my **Father's** business?*" Yes, **Jesus** did know who His **Heavenly Father** was at this time.

Chapter 2

Please let me skip over at this time to the fourth book of the New Testament, the book of the gospel of the beloved John. John was a young teenager at the time of the three-year ministry of **Jesus**. John was not only one of the twelve selected men to be His disciples, but he was the one whom **Jesus** loved as His favorite. He was the one who at the **Lord**'s last supper leaned back on the **Lord**'s breast and showed His love.

I had no intentions of skipping around in the writing of the New Testament, but to go right on through the book of Matthew. But last night the precious **Holy Ghost** woke me up to say to the ears of my heart, "John David, I want you to go now to the scriptures of John 1:1" *"In the beginning was the Word,* (**Jesus**) *and the Word was with God; and the Word was God."* (John 1:2) *"The same was in the beginning with God.*

(John 1:12) *"But as many as did received Him, to them gave He power to become the sons of God, even to them that believe on His name."*

Now you will read in John 1:14: *"And the Word* (**Jesus**) *was made flesh, and dwelt among us,* (and we beheld His glory, the glory as of the only begotten son of the **Father**) *full of grace and truth."*

As I said from the very first start of writing this book, it would be written by the persuasion of the **Holy Ghost**, and it is with that persuasion that I have skipped around and written the above scriptures.

Now let us go back to Matthew where John the Baptist was preaching in the wilderness. John the Baptist said as he was baptizing the sinners who were coming to him. (Matthew 3:11) *"I indeed baptize you with water unto repentance: but He that cometh after me is mightier than I, whose shoes I am not worthy to bear; He shall baptize you with the **Holy Ghost** and with fire."*

Chapter 3

I am being led again to skip to the book of Acts. In Acts 2:1-4: *"And when the day of Pentecost was fully come, they were all with one accord in one place. And suddenly there came a sound from heaven as of a mighty wind, and it filled all the house where they were sitting. And there appeared unto them cloven tongues like as of fire and it sat upon each of them. And they were all filled with the **Holy Ghost** and began to speak with other tongues, as the Spirit gave them utterance."*

The book of Acts was written by Luke, the Physician, and it was written about sixty four years after John the Baptist made this statement in Matthew 3:11 where he said **Jesus** will baptize you with the **Holy Ghost** and with fire.

At the day of Pentecost, **Jesus** (our **Salvation**) had gone back to heaven and was standing at the right hand of **God** the **Father** and had sent the **Comforter**, who is the **Holy Ghost**. (John 14:26) *"But the **Comforter**, which is the **Holy Ghost**, whom the **Father** will send in my name, He shall teach you all things, and bring things to remembrance, whatsoever I have said unto you."*

What I am trying to do is show you, the reader, how **God's** Holy Bible will tie all scriptures together to prove every one of the scriptures to be true. This is the Holy Word of **God**. Amen.

The Great Reunion

Chapter 4

Let's go back to the book of Matthew as we see **Jesus** coming to John to be baptized by Him. But John knew, who **Jesus** was and that He was the Salvation sent from **God** to rescue us from our sins and from great danger. That is why John said, "No **Lord** not that I baptize you, but that you baptize me." John knew that **Jesus** was without sin and had no reason to be baptized unto repentance.

Jesus answered John: (Matthew 3:15) *"Suffer it to be so now: for thus it becometh us to fulfill all righteousness."* I believe that the righteousness that **Jesus** was speaking of at this time was the righteousness that all men must have in order to get into heaven. I believe **Jesus** was setting us an example for us to go by with the symbolism of the type of baptism that was to be (total submersion). And I also believe that He was also taking the place of the thief on the cross and the men of war who have received **Jesus** and are killed before they can be baptized in water. Also, there are those on their deathbed who receive **Jesus** as their Salvation and are unable to get to water to be baptized. Also those who have gone to the alter and confessed the **Lord** and asked to be baptized and become a member of **God's** church and, having to wait for a week or two before baptism can be done, are killed in the meantime or die of natural causes.

(Matthew 3:16-17) *"And **Jesus** when He was baptized, went up straightway* (after total submersion) *out of the water: and, low, the heavens were opened* unto Him, and He saw the **Spirit** of **God** descending like a dove and lighting upon Him. And lo a voice from heaven, saying, this is my **Beloved Son**, in whom I am well pleased." **Jesus** did receive **God's Holy Spirit** at this very time; and **God's Spirit** led Him into the wilderness and He fasted for forty days and forty nights.

It is amazing to me how **Jesus** stood so strong against the tempter – the devil. But He did it with Satan himself, challenging **Jesus** with great temptations. At this time, when **Jesus** was at His weakest from fasting, Satan took Him on a high mountain and showed Him (**Jesus**) all the kingdoms of the world and the glory of them. I believe Satan showed Him all of the cities at that time and their glory and all of the cities of the future such as Las Vegas, U.S.A.; Monte Carlo; Paris, France; London, England. But **Jesus** would say in Matthew 4:10, "*Get thee hence, Satan; for it is written, Thou shalt worship the* **Lord** *thy* **God**; *and Him only shalt thou serve.*" This put the devil on the run because he knew in **Jesus**, he had more than he could handle.

And something to remember, **Jesus** was a man of flesh and blood and bones, just like His disciples. But **Jesus** prevailed and did not fail against Satan.

After the temptation the angels came and ministered to **Jesus**. I would like to think that these ministering angles did caress Him and were saying all is going to be all right, **Jesus, Great Son** of **God**.

In reading the rest of Chapter four of Matthew, we can see that **Jesus** went to Capernaum to live and from there He started gathering His twelve chosen disciples, making ready for His public ministry.

Chapter 5

In Matthew, Chapter 5 **Jesus** began to preach His first sermon to the multitude of the people. That sermon became known as "The Sermon on the Mount". At that time He preached on subjects such as righteousness, swearing, praying, forgiveness, and blessings of all types, such as health, financial, faith, and treasures in heaven. Finally He said: (Matthew 6:33) *"But seek ye first the **Kingdom** of **God**, and His righteousness: and all these things shall be added unto you."*

When **Jesus** finished preaching this sermon, He began to go His way with His disciples. There came a man who had been listening to His sermon and as he came, he worshipped Him saying, "**Lord**, I have leprosy, I am a leper, but I know if you want to, you can heal me." Then **Jesus** said to the leper, "I will, be thou clean." And immediately the leper was cleansed. This was the first miraculous healing that **Jesus** did that Matthew wrote about. Turning the water into wine at a wedding was the first miracle, but He would do many more as He walked the road of His ministry for three years.

One of the best-known miracles **Jesus** did was the calming of the sea even with the wind howling as a roaring lion and the ship almost covered with the waves. **Jesus** and His disciples were crossing the Sea of Galilee. **Jesus**, being tired from preaching and teaching, was worn out and was fast asleep. His disciples came to Him and said, "**Lord**, don't you care that the ship is about to sink and we all will drown?" Then **Jesus** said in Matthew 8:25: *"Why are ye fearful, O ye of little faith?"* I can imagine

The Great Reunion

how fearful and amazed the disciples were when **Jesus** stood up and shouted 'Peace, be still' and the wind laid and obeyed Him and the sea became as clear glass. (Matthew 8:27) *"But the men marveled, saying, what manner of man is this, that even the winds and the sea obey Him"* Yes, our **Master** had the faith to even calm the sea and He gave us that same faith.

One day as **Jesus** was by the sea preaching, there came one of the rulers named Jairus, of the synagogues saying to **Jesus**, "My twelve year old daughter is sick and is dying. Will you please come and lay your hands on her that she may be healed and not die?" **Jesus** said to this man, "Yes, I will come with you." And as they started to go to Jairus' house many people followed Him.

(Mark 5:25-26) *"And a certain woman, which had an issue of blood twelve years. And had suffered many things of many physicians, and had spent all that she had, and was nothing bettered, but rather grew worse."*

This woman had heard of all the miracles **Jesus** had done to heal the sick and she knew He was the answer to her sickness, without a doubt. As this woman came up behind **Jesus** she began to work her way through all the people and all the while she was thinking and saying to, herself, "If I can but touch the hem of his robe, I shall be healed of this blood issue." When she finally got close enough, she reached out and touched the hem of his robe. Immediately the issue of her blood flow stopped and she knew it. She had no doubt.

And **Jesus** immediately felt that virtue go out of Him and turned about and said, "Who touched my clothes?" The woman was afraid and trembling knowing what she had done. (Mark 5:34) *"And He said unto her, Daughter, thy faith hath made thee whole; go in peace, and be whole of thy plague."*

I believe this miraculous healing was also done for another persons benefit. Because at that very time, a certain one came from Jairus' house telling Jairus that his daughter had already died. **Jesus** said to Jairus, "Be not afraid, and only believe. They continued on to Jairus' house. I can imagine how it made Jairus' wife feel with all the weeping going on when Jairus walked in with **Jesus** and said to his wife, "I have brought the healer for my daughter. (Mark 5:39) *"And when He (**Jesus**) had come in, He saith unto them, why make ye this ado, and weep? The damsel is not dead, but sleepeth."*

The people that were there laughed, scorning **Jesus**. So **Jesus** put them all out except Peter, James and John the brother of James. Then He took the father and mother of the girl and entered where she was. **Jesus** took the girl by the hand and said unto her, "Damsel, I say unto thee, arise." And she did. Then **Jesus** told Jairus and his wife to feed her and don't tell anyone about this, and they were astonished.

I can see Jarius telling his wife about seeing the woman with the issue of blood healed while on their way to his house. And that is how he kept the faith and believed that **Jesus** could also make their daughter arise.

Dear Reader, let me ask you at this time, do you have an issue of any kind that you need to bring to the **Healer**, the **Master**, the **Lord** of **Salvation**? Are you trying to put this issue off until it passes away? Let me say, don't do that! The **Holy Spirit** that **Jesus** sent to be your

Comforter and your helper is right now available to come into your precious soul and live with your own **God-given** spirit. And because they are in agreement, they can take charge of that issue and settle it right now. If you will only believe and not doubt, but have faith, that issue can be healed right now. Right now accept **Jesus** as your personal **Lord** and **Savior**. Let Him put that issue behind you just as He did for these two who came to Him.

Let me give you an example where the writer wrote that **Jesus** said (Matthew 7:7) *"Ask, and it shall be given you; seek, and you shall find; knock, and it shall be opened unto you."* **God** wants to give unto you. That is why He sent His **Son** from heaven to say these things to you. **Jesus** wants first to give you **Salvation**. He wants to rescue you from great danger. The very first thing you must do is to receive it, and then you will qualify for all the rest of His gifts.

(Matthew 7:11) *"If ye then, being evil, know how to give good gifts unto your children, how much more shall your Father which is in heaven give good things to them that ask Him."* Now this is not me speaking or Matthew speaking, but this is **Jesus** saying these things.

(Matthew 10:32-33) *"But whosoever therefore shall confess Me before men, Him will I also confess before My Father which is in heaven. But whosoever shall deny Me before men, him will I also deny before My Father which is in heaven."* To me, that makes it pretty plain and simple to understand. We either confess or deny **Jesus**. There is just not any in between with **Jesus**. He gives you one of two choices, deny or confess.

Chapter 6

What can we do but believe what the Holy Word of **God** says? As I have said before, I do believe The Holy Bible as the written **Word** of **God**. I believe every word to be true. And if I am wrong, which I am not, what do I have to lose? Nothing. But if I am right, and I am, what do you have to lose. If you believe not, you have everything to lose. The options are simple: eternal damnation if you do not believe in **Jesus**; Eternity with **God** if you accept His only begotten Son, **Jesus**.

So now let us go see why **God** sent His **Son**. (John 3:15-16) *"That whosoever* (that is you and me) *believeth in Him should not perish, but have eternal life. For* **God** *so loved the world, that He gave His only begotten* **Son***, that whosoever* (again you and me) *believeth in Him should not perish, but have everlasting life."*

This was the covenant that was made before man was ever created, when **God** the **Father**, and **Christ** the **Son**, and the **Holy Ghost** stood on that hill of Glory and looked over everything that had been created, except man, and the three **Godheads** were in one accord and said, "Let us make man in our image."

I am so grateful that my **Heavenly Father** loved me so much that he would give His **Son's** life in order that I could keep mine for eternity. And I am so happy and glad when I think about how on April 1975, **Jesus** came to me and said to the ears of my heart, "John David, I will trade you my righteousness for your sins." Very quickly I said, "OK **Lord**, trade." Then as I began to confess my sins to Him, I began to think to myself, but

The Great Reunion

that sin is not that much, so I same as said to myself, I get so much pleasure out of that one, I'll just keep that one. **That won't work with Jesus.**

After all of my confessing of my sins that I wanted Him to take from me, and keeping just a few of the small ones, **Jesus** said to the ears of my heart, "Are you through confessing?" I said, "Yes. **Lord** that is all." At that the **Lord** said to ears of my heart, "No deal! I said I would trade my righteousness for your sins; all of your sins, and I don't do a partial package deal." I said, weeping and at this time knowing that I was dying because I was very sick, "**Lord** I give you all of my sins, I surrender all." **Jesus** accepted them and gave me His righteousness for my sins. Amen.

You see, when we pray, we must give up everything and be willing to let the **Holy Spirit** have **His way** and let Him change us. If we try to do our own changing, we will goof it up just trying.

In John 14:6 **Jesus** plainly tells us when He spoke to Thomas: "*I am the way, the truth, and the life: No man cometh unto the **Father**, but by Me.*"

That makes it pretty simple. If you want to go to the **Father** you are going to have to go by way of **Jesus**. There is no other way. But He has got His door open to you. What it boils down to is if you believe the Bible, then you know this scripture is the truth. **No other way.**

Where does man fit into **God's** plan? Was man made a little lower than the angels? Yes, he was. First let us go to Psalm 8:5: "*For thou hast made Him a little lower than the angels, and hast crowned Him with glory and honor.*"

(Hebrews 2:7) *"Thou madest Him a little lower than the angels; thou crowndst Him with glory and honor, and didst set Him over the works of thy hands."*

As Divine as **Christ** was, He was also as human as you and I because in Hebrews 2:9, we read: *"But we see **Jesus**, who was made a little lower than the angels for the suffering of death, crowned with glory and honor; that He by the grace of **God** should taste death for every man."*

Think about this. **God's** angels don't die. That is why the angels who were rebellious with Lucifer, the devil, are at the end times to be chained and then thrown to the bottomless pit of hell for all eternity.

Christ Jesus had to die for man's Salvation. (Hebrews 2:17) *"Wherefore in all things it behoved Him to be made like unto His brethren, that He might be a merciful and faithful high priest in things pertaining to **God**, to make reconciliation for the sins of the people."*

(Hebrews 2:18) *"For in that He Himself hath suffered being tempted He is able to succour them that are tempted."* **Jesus**, yes, He does understand for He was **God** and took on human form.

So we can see **Jesus** for a short time of thirty-three years was made a little lower than angels for one purpose. That was for dying on the cross.

Let me go by scripture and prove my point. This writing needs to be thoroughly understood that **God** did not kill the rebellious angels that sinned. But He cast them down to hell and delivered them into chains of darkness to be reserved unto Judgment.

You see when the angels were created, they were

created not to die; where man was created to die if he broke the covenant **God** made with him which was not to eat the forbidden fruit of one certain tree. Amen.

Chapter 7

Now since **God** has raised **Jesus** from the dead and He is at **God's** right hand in His glorified body, all things, including angels, are under and are subject to Him. (I Peter 3:22) *"Who is gone into heaven, and is on the right hand of **God**; angels and authorities and powers being made subject unto Him."*

Let me move into I Timothy 2: 5: *"For there is one **God**, and one mediator between **God** and men, the man Christ **Jesus**."*

He is right now ready to give to our **Heavenly Father** the papers for our adoption, which are signed with His precious blood. Are you ready to receive that adoption? Are you ready to say, "I give up? I totally and unconditionally surrender." Do it right now! Years without **Jesus** are wasted years. He is the power of heaven and also of earth.

As I have said it was not my intention to jump around in the scriptures going from one book to another, but that is what the **Holy Ghost** has persuaded me to do, so I know you will get a much better writing and a better understanding if I let Him lead me in these writings.

I could go on from one scripture to another telling of the many wonderful miracles that **Jesus** did that are registered in all twenty-seven books of the New Testament. But as I said from the beginning of writing from the Old Testament, it all started six thousand years ago when the prophets started telling of His coming and of the last and final covenant between **God** the **Father**, **Christ** the **Son**, and the **Holy Ghost**. The covenant is

The Great Reunion

the **Son's** death on the cross and the spilling of His blood so that all who would believe could be saved and be in **God's** great Reunion in heaven.

At this time I feel I am being persuaded by the **Holy Ghost** to give and write these scriptures to you, the Reader: **God's** plan for your Salvation. (Rescue from great danger).

(Acts 2:21) "And it shall come to pass; that *whosoever shall call on the name of the* **Lord** *shall be saved.*"

(Acts 3:28) "*Then Peter said unto them, Repent,* (be sorrowful) *and be baptized every one of you in the name of* **Jesus Christ** *for the remission of sins, and you shall receive the gift of the* **Holy Ghost.**"

(Acts 16:31) "*and they said, believe on the* **Lord Jesus** *Christ, and thou shalt be saved, and thy house.*"

(Romans 10:9) "*That if thou shalt confess with thy mouth the* **Lord Jesus** *and shalt believe in thine heart that* **God** *hath raised him from the dead, thou shalt be saved.*"

(Romans 10:13) "*For whosoever shall call upon the name of the* **Lord** *shall be saved.*"

(Romans 6:23) "*For the wages of sin is death; but the gift of* **God** *is eternal life through* **Jesus** *Christ our* **Lord**.*"

(Ephesians 2:8-9) "*For by grace are ye saved through faith; and that not of yourselves; it is the gift of* **God**. *Not of works, lest any man should boast.*"

Chapter 8

I was brand new into reading the **Word** of **God** – the Bible. I was no more than sixty days acquainted with what it was saying to me, when I ran across this scripture. (Acts 2:21) I had to read it over several times with much praying as I read.

I began to think to myself, "Is **God** willing to forgive me of all of my past sins? Everyone of these past sins?" And with that thought in mind one of the most evil sins of my eight years of life flashed through my mind. One of our little female dogs had given birth to six new puppies. And as I began to pick one up and pet the puppy, my little female fearful that I was going to do harm to her pups, made a snapping bite at me. It is only natural that any mother would protect her pups under these circumstances. It was a natural reaction for her to do it. But anger crept up in my mind as I said to myself, "I'll show you what you get when you try to bite me."

I picked up a club and beat the mother dog until it was dead. Afterwards, I realized that the pups needed their mother's feedings. So I took each pup and drowned all six puppies in a tub of water. Then realizing what I had done, I took them and buried them. This was so when the family members asked, what happened to the little dog and her puppies, I would say, "I don't know" And lie about it.

As I thought more about this sin, I started weeping bitterly and asking the **Lord** to please forgive me of this sin that I have carried in my mind for the past thirty years. The **Holy Spirit** answered that question, "Yes,

The Great Reunion

now that you have confessed it as a sin that was against the little dog and against me. John David, **God** has, through the spilled blood of His **Son**, now forgiven you of that sin in the name of **Jesus**."

Then (Acts 16:31) was brought to my mind as the **Lord's Spirit** said to the ears of my own heart. "Yes, John David, I not only will forgive you, I will also save you! I'll give you salvation." (Meaning, rescue from great danger). And the ears of my heart seemed to hear him say, "Not only will I do this for you, but I will do it for all your household as well and bring all of them with you to my own great meeting – "The Great Reunion." Amen.

Next (Romans 10:9) spoke to my heart as I began to speak with my tongue that is the speaker for my soul; as I said, "Yes, **Lord**, I do believe without any reservation that my **Savior**, **Jesus Christ**, did die for me and all my sins. And after His death He was placed into a burial tomb for three days, and after three days **God** raised Him from the dead. And this very day, He is alive and at **God's** right hand side and now intercedes for me as I pray to you, **My Father**."

Going back to Romans 6:23, I saw from the actions of my past life the sinfulness that was by my own choice and by my own doings. My rightful wage should be eternal death. But **God** with his Grace, His complete love, had a gift that He wanted to give me that was already bought and paid for by His only begotten **Son, Jesus Christ**.

Ephesians 2: 8-9 immediately flashed before my mind and later it would come to my heart that **God**'s amazing grace, His complete love, would be followed up by my

A Road That Won't Travel

own faith that he had given me as a gift. He has given it to you with the same measure.

That faith is the unmerited favor of **God**. It is something that you cannot buy. All that is required is that you accept it whole-heartedly, believing and without doubt. Yes, **God** wants you to have a full measure of faith. **God** is not a partially giving **God**, nor is He with partiality of one over another. **God** will give you just as much faith, wisdom, knowledge and understanding as all of the understandings that He gave the King Solomon in I Kings, Chapter 3. But, you must by faith accept it to receive it.

Skipping all the way to Hebrews 2:9 I read where my **Lord** and **Savior**, **Christ Jesus**, the **Holy Jewel** of heaven, came here to earth to be born of a virgin woman and to be made a little lower than the angels in order to die to erase man's sins. Amen.

Yes, all of my sins and yours are now covered by His willing choice to be a sacrifice for all our sins. It is already bought and paid for. All we must do is accept and receive it. It is now our choice. My own choice is to be at this "Great Reunion". What is yours?

Think about this! **God**, Himself killed His own animal creature, and shed the animal's blood to cover the sin of Adam and Eve. That is why our **God** demanded that there be a blood and death sacrifice as payment for all of Man's sins. Read Genesis 3:21: *"Unto Adam also and to his wife did the **Lord God** make coats of skins and clothed them."* This was the red thread that would be all the way through the Bible.

Looking back I can see how it must have hurt our

Creator (God) to have to kill one of the creatures He created. Even though, He was willing to do it for His most prized creations man and woman. Yes, He was justified in what He did! I was not. But despite being completely unjustified, He was still willing to forgive me. Why? He always loves me just that much, even as He loves you.

I am so grateful that **God** has shown how much He loves us all that He would allow His only **Son** to die on the Cross so that He could give us this gift of eternal life and bring us to His own "Great Reunion". My question still is, "Will you be there at the "The Great Reunion?" I certainly hope so.

I do know that many of the scriptures in this book have not been explained and there is a reason for that. Dear Reader, the **Comforter** which is the **Holy Ghost** which **Jesus** sent after His return to His holy home in heaven has said to the ears of my heart, "There are some of these scriptures that I (The **Holy Ghost**) want to teach them. I want to give them the gift of understanding and the holy wisdom of knowing what they need; such as the holy healing that is still today as it was 2000 years ago. That was when **Jesus** allowed the soldier of Pilate to whip Him and put those thirty nine stripes upon His body." Yes, **Jesus** is willing today as He was then to give you that healing power. Will you be at "The Great Reunion?"

Chapter 9

Dear Reader, remain patient while you are reading for this too is a gift. The **Holy Spirit** cannot enter unto a heart that is disturbed with unbelief. Now if you will turn to your Bible and read Mark 9:24 about when this man that was seeking a favor of **Jesus** did see the results.

Let me offer a suggestion when you read your Bible. Go to a private place, if possible, and pray for an understanding before you ever start reading. This does work in your favor and **God** will hear whatsoever you are praying. Amen.

What it boils down to is this. If you read your Bible you will know this scripture is truth. No other way. **God** does not make exceptions. And above all, **God** cannot and will not lie.

Let me move into 1 Timothy 2:15: *"For there is* **One God**, *and* **One Mediator** *between* **God** *and men, the man* **Christ Jesus**.*"*

(1 John 4:15) *"Whosoever* (you and me) *shall confess that* **Jesus** *is the* **Son** *of* **God**, **God** *dwelleth in Him, and He in* **God**.*"*

(1 John 5:12) *"He that hath the* **Son** *hath life; and He that hath not the* **Son** *of* **God** *hath not life."*

(1 John 5:7) *"For there are three that bear record in heaven, the* **Father**, *the* **Word**, *and the* **Holy Ghost**: *and these three are one."*

Now please let me back up to Matthew 28:19: *"Go ye therefore, and teach all nations, baptizing them in the name of the* **Father**, *and of the* **Son**, *and of the* **Holy Ghost**.*"* These are the three.

Dear Reader, if you can accept these scriptures as the **Holy Ghost** has given to me to write, then you do qualify for the following scriptures.

(I Peter 2:24) *"Who His own self bare our sins in His own body on the tree, which we, being dead to sins, should live unto righteousness: by whose stripes ye were healed."*

(Mark 11:24) *"Therefore, I say unto you, (you and me) What things soever ye desire, when ye pray, believe that ye receive them, and ye shall have them."* **God** is not a **God** that will say to you, "No, you don't need that."

(John 14:13-14) *"And whatsoever ye shall ask in my name, that will I do, that the* **Father** *may be glorified in the* **Son**. *If ye shall ask anything in my name, I will do it."*

Chapter 10

Well, there it is and all for your asking. Receive and accept **Jesus** this very hour. That is the very first thing you must do in order to qualify for all of His blessings.

This book has been written with the very persuasion of the **Holy Ghost**. It is in my dearest prayer to the **Lord** that you will receive it in that very way and receive it right now. Don't wait until it is too late.

In closing, let me say to you: be baptized and go to the church of your choice. Read **God's Holy Word** every day for at least fifteen minutes. It is **God's** way of talking to you, just as he talked to Moses through the burning bush. The Holy Bible is how he will speak to you. Just listen with the ears of your heart open.

EXPECT A MIRACLE ! It is on its way.

Remember Always: God loves you, and so do I.

The finishing touch to this book is

"A Road That Won't Travel"

It was written at the direction of the **Holy Spirit**.

Please, read it with a prayerful heart and an open mind.

A Road That Won't Travel!

DANGER!!

JOHN DAVID WHITEHEAD......

The Great Reunion

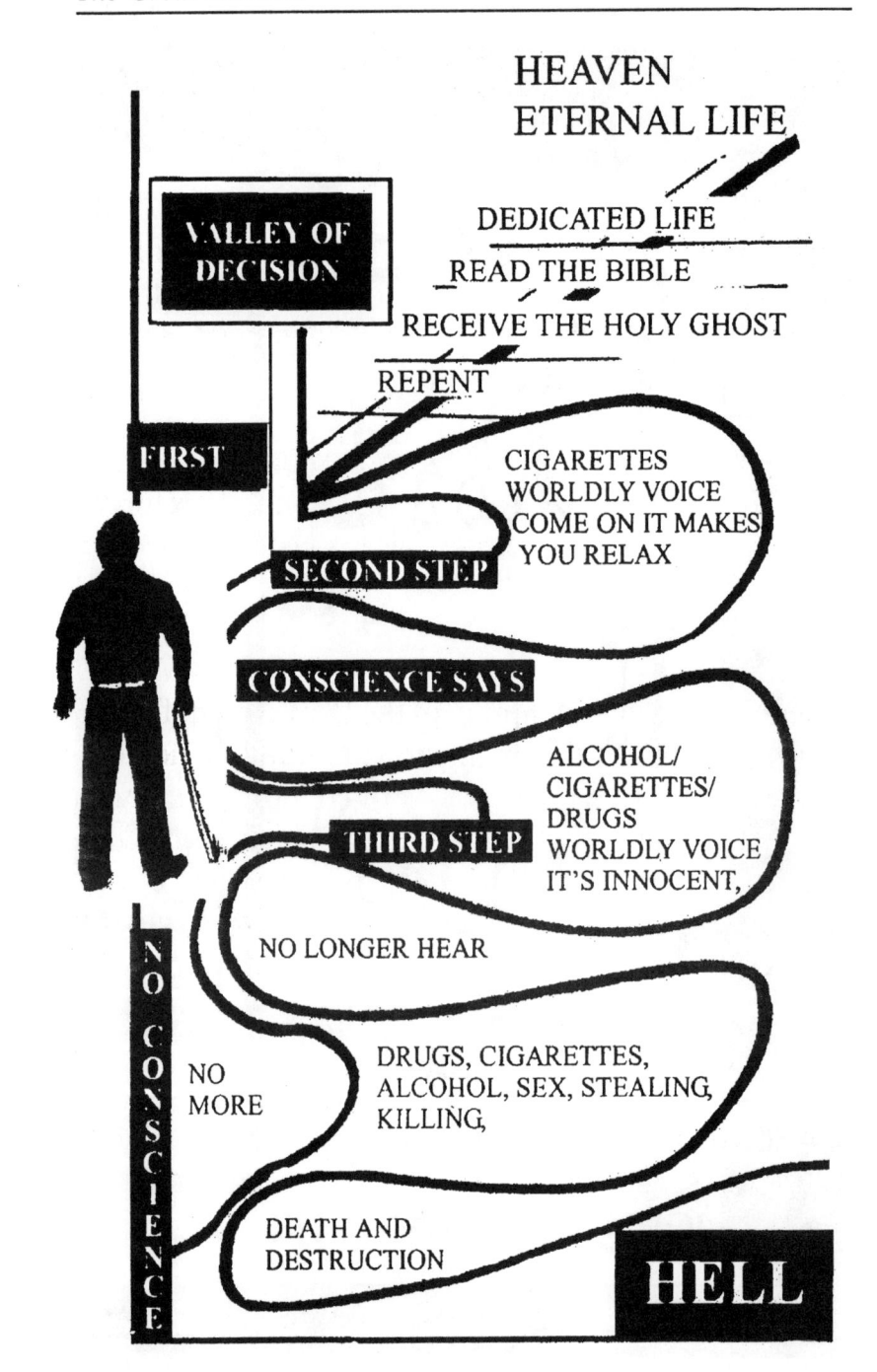

HEAVEN
ETERNAL LIFE

VALLEY OF DECISION

DEDICATED LIFE

READ THE BIBLE

RECEIVE THE HOLY GHOST

REPENT

FIRST

CIGARETTES
WORLDLY VOICE
COME ON IT MAKES
YOU RELAX

SECOND STEP

CONSCIENCE SAYS

ALCOHOL/
CIGARETTES/
DRUGS
WORLDLY VOICE
IT'S INNOCENT,

THIRD STEP

NO LONGER HEAR

NO CONSCIENCE

NO MORE

DRUGS, CIGARETTES, ALCOHOL, SEX, STEALING, KILLING,

DEATH AND DESTRUCTION

HELL

FOREWORD

While writing this little book, I was reminded of the time I was invited to church by my Aunt, my mother's sister. The church was Thirty Second and High Baptist Church and I was ten years old.

The Pastor, Harvey Hicks, preached a powerful sermon on the Five Steps of Salvation. I will never forget this preacher or his sermon. It was the last time I would receive the coaching of the **Holy Spirit** for thirty years.

With that in mind, I say to you, "DON'T WAIT." When you feel the prompting of the **Holy Spirit**, follow His instructions at that moment. It's with this memory that I wish to say, no matter how old or how young you are, don't let the **Holy Spirit** sent by **Jesus** from **God** pass you by. It's His choice to sweep the sins out of your life and live within your Soul. I let Him have that choice. He is life eternal.

§ § §

This is written with the intention of giving my **Lord** and Savior **Jesus** thanks for his eternal Love for **God**, The **Father**, and for me.

-- John David Whitehead

INTRODUCTION

A Road That Won't Travel! was written by a man who went through the very pits of hell before **God** could get his attention. The devil tried to take his life at a very young age, but **God** would not permit him to have it.

As a young child, John David Whitehead was looking for love in all the wrong places, trying to fit in with the other children who were raised up in the city. But he was always looked down upon because of his country ways, ragged clothes, and worn out shoes. This made him resentful and he felt like he had to prove himself.

Unknowingly, all this time John David was being led by the devil, who was always trying to destroy him, but **God** had a plan for John David's life. **God** wanted a soul winner, someone who would stand in the face of the enemy against all odds and come through in victory. The devil had him thinking he deserved eternal hell. That's how bad the enemy can deceive those who allow him to.

This book will help open the eyes of parents whose children are being put through peer pressure at school to do drugs, tobacco and alcohol. Become your child's best friend and know when the red flag is raised because the enemy is always trying to destroy them.

I highly recommend this book for all young people and parents alike.

THANK YOU John David for sharing your life. I know it was very hard, and it was not easy seeing your beloved wife and son going through hell because of your mistakes.

— *Farrell Clements*

Chapter 1

I was born on a dusty cotton field road, in a four room, "shot-gun house" in the area of Scott, Arkansas. I was the fifth child of Edward and Johnnie Whitehead. They named me "John David". My mother later told me she chose the name for it's meaning, "BELOVED, GIFT OF GOD."

Many years later, I walked on "Troubled Waters", many miles in the ways of Satan. It was brought to my mind many times, was I a "gift from **God**" or had the devil found a way to send a man here on earth to do the wickedness, "which I was doing?"

I was hooked on tobacco by the time I was seven years old. That would be the start of my getting high with an altered mind and it would last for another forty years. Dad and Mother had lived in dire poverty trying to raise a family in those cotton fields. I was about nine years old when Dad moved us off the farm and into the city. I look back and I see and hear the words I spoke so long ago. "I WISH I HAD NEVER BEEN BORN!" **God** in His mercy heard me, but unknown to me then, He had a plan for me.

Moving to Little Rock, I found out very fast that things were very different for a "country boy" coming to town. I had much resentment because I was "looked down on" by the other children in my school. Being in a "move around family", five different schools in my first two years in Little Rock also affected me. I became very aggressive toward other children, my teachers, and staff members. By the time I had reached the sixth grade,

The Great Reunion

I had become known as the toughest boy in school, and would fight at the drop of a hat. I do believe the principal of the school actually hated me. I got thirty to forty whippings while in the sixth grade. The staff never looked to see "WHAT'S HIS PROBLEM" and by this time I surely had one. I was getting drunk at least twice a week.

After finishing the seventh grade, I got sick due to smoking cigarette butts that I picked up from the street gutter. I spent thirty days in the hospital and was diagnosed as having an enlarged heart caused by tuberculosis. At that time T.B., as it was known, was not curable, and like cancer is now, it was a killer. So I was sent to the State T.B. Sanatorium, at Booneville, Arkansas, one hundred miles away from my family. I was there for one year. It was a terrible time. After missing an entire year of school, I simply refused to go back. Then I became what is now called a "street child." I was drinking and doping and losing all contact with reality. I would think to myself, "I'm fourteen years old, I'll do my own thing." I can look back now and see that when my eighteenth birthday came and I enlisted in the U. S. Army, my mother must have thought "THANK GOD" now that he has someone to take care of him. What she didn't know was that I was now a confirmed alcoholic and drug addict. The Army sent me to Germany, and it was there I began to get into drug trafficking, and got to be known as the base drug dealer. After getting caught five times drugged up and drunk, I was court marshaled, given three months in the stockade, and then sent home with a general UNDESIRABLE discharge. This still haunts me to this day.

Getting out of the army, I was in a daze and somehow ended up in Broadview, Illinois, a suburb of Chicago. I went to work for a company as an owner/operator truck driver. I stayed in this work with the same company for about ten years. During this time I met and married my wife, Barbara and we had three children: David, Donna and Doyen. She was and still is a fine lady.

After I got into my thirties, I realized how I had totally given up on my responsibilities as a husband and father. I got deep into drugs and alcohol and had centered my whole life around those two things. I was a drug dealer from the age of twenty-one. Now I was known to the criminal activist as, "if you need to get it moved, see John David." This reputation would stick with me even to the age of thirty-eight. At that time, I was caught and busted with the largest amount of marijuana in Arkansas. That was 1973. I went to court and lied like a dog and still I was found guilty and sentenced to five years in the Arkansas State Prison, Cummins unit.

One day, I came in from the fields from hoeing onions and there on my bunk lay a Bible. Until this day, I do not know who put it there. I began to read it. I had never read a Bible before this time. I read it for about thirty days before it began to make sense to me. I saw in this book where I was "lost" because I was "without salvation."

My actions over the past twenty-five years had put me in all 48 states, and in every city with a population of over one hundred thousand. I had spent at least one night in every city drugged up, drunk and committing adultery. I saw a re-run of these things in my mind. I now understood that my actions were against **God Almighty's** love for me and that Satan had been walking hand in hand with me those twenty-five years. YES, the Bible, **God's** Holy Word, was preparing me for what would come next.

    I was working on what is called the long line, which is a group of twenty-six men, who line up in the field on twenty-six rows of onions, cotton, or whatever that was being grown. This day we were hoeing onions. As we hoed through the field, I became sick and started throwing up blood. An ulcer I had had for many years had perforated and within a few minutes my white uniform was blood red. Still I wasn't allowed to stop hoeing. There are three long line riders on horseback with high-powered rifles guarding the long line. One of those guards saw that I was sick and he called to the other two guards by radio saying, "I'm going to take this man back to the prison." First, I have never seen a man taken out of the fields for any reason, IT WAS NEVER HEARD OF. The guard put me in front of his horse and literally ran me the full mile back to the prison.

    Upon arriving at the prison yard, I was taken to the desk, which is the inside prison control center. The officer who was on duty this day was known as "The Devil." When he saw how I was throwing up blood on the floor, the center control officer began to swear and curse me with names that are unprintable. He told me, "Whitehead, go on back to your dormitory and wait until I figure out what to do with you." I knew this officer hated inmates and his hope was I would die that very day. I went into

A Road That Won't Travel

my dormitory. It was set up to house one hundred twenty-five, but at this time it was over crowded with two hundred and twelve men. As I entered the dormitory, I noticed there was no one in the dormitory, not even the orderly. I had never seen this before. I walked to my bunk and I picked up a five-gallon spit bucket that the tobacco chewers used. I used it to throw up the blood that I was losing. After I lay down on my bunk for a few minutes, I began to tremble from the loss of blood. I began to realize I was dying, and worse than that, I realized I would be in Hell tomorrow. Yes, I now knew and believed there was a "hell" from reading the Bible, **God's** Holy Word. And from that reading, I came to realize that due to my lifetime actions of sin, drunkenness, doping, whore mongering, fornication, transgressions, those sins of my life that flashed before my eyes, I deserved Hell. I began to panic, telling **Jesus** that I'm sorry; I won't do it any more. Then I began to tell Him, "If you will heal me, I'll give witness to everyone, everywhere I go." The **Lord** wasn't buying it. I actually heard a spiritual voice say, "I'm not your mother, nor am I your wife, so stop lying to me and seek you the Kingdom of **God** and His righteousness." Just as surely as King Belshazzar, in the fifth chapter of the book of Daniel, saw the writing on the wall, so did I see the writing on the dormitory wall saying, "Seek the Kingdom of **God** and His Righteousness."

I became frightened and began to say, "**Lord**, please help me." But still the **Lord** wasn't buying it. I was waving a white flag of surrender and still He wasn't buying it. I said to the **Comforter** whom **Jesus** sent me, "Please,

The Great Reunion

Holy Ghost tell **Jesus** I'm sorry." At that he said, "No, you tell Him." I began to weep bitterly, just as Peter did (Matt. 26:75) saying, "**Lord,** you forgave Peter, why not me?" Still nothing. As I slid off my bunk and kneeled beside the bed in my own blood that had splattered over the spit bucket, I began to cry out to the **Lord,** saying, "I don't blame you, I wouldn't want to have a person like me in heaven with you either; telling Him, I see all the things that are not of you and against you". I said, "I deserve exactly what I will be getting, Eternal Hell." Then I said, "I just want you to know I am truly sorry for the things I have done against you and I do apologize to you." Before I got that sentence finished, **Jesus** Saved Me. Through the Grace and Mercy of **God Almighty**, I knew I was saved at that instant.

You see, at first I was waving a white flag of Surrender, but it was a flag of partial surrender and under my own conditions. Now I was waving a bloody red flag; red with the blood of **Jesus.**

Now I was asking for no conditions, but I was giving 100% of me. Now I was willing to do an unconditional total surrender. Now, **Jesus** was willing to accept my surrender and give me salvation. He rescued me from great danger.

Now, he was accepting what He had already bought and paid for at Calvary – MY ETERNAL SOUL. Amen!! Hallelujah!!

I lay on my bunk for about thirty minutes just thanking my **Savior** for my salvation – my rescue from great danger. I thanked Him over and over. Amen!! Hallelujah!!!

As I began to talk to my **Lord** saying, "OK, **Lord,**

now I am ready to die", but the **Holy Spirit** spoke to me and said: "You've got work to do. Go tell the security officer about you being born again and the salvation you now have, and I will give you other words to say."

At that, I walked out of the dormitory and walked up to the yard desk officer, and began to tell him I was now saved, born again. I told him "if you want to be, you can be saved too." Then I said, "not only have I been saved, I have been healed; I can outwork any man in the field." At that the officer looked at the Sergeant and said, "Get the prison van and take this S.O.B. to the state hospital at Little Rock. He has gone completely crazy."

Arriving at the hospital, the doctors began to take tests and at the end they said, "Well, with his blood count so low, he has surely lost a great deal of blood." My blood count was dangerously low, but I would not take treatment. The very next day on a recheck of my blood count, the doctors stood back and said, "Unbelievable, it's completely normal." At that, I said, "Just proof that **Jesus** is still healing," just as he did 2000 years ago. Amen!! Hallelujah!!

I was held in the hospital for thirty days before I was cleared as being healed. Upon my return to the prison, I was told the warden had recommended that I be given early release and sent home. My last month was a month of studying the Bible and getting me ready to be a walking witness for the **Lord and Savior, Jesus.**

The Great Reunion

Chapter 2

I was paroled in 1976 and kept close to the **Lord** until 1979. At that time I was convinced I could run a business and be very successful. My brother Jim ended up investing two hundred fifty thousand dollars in the business and me. He lost it all within the next two years.

In 1981, I became sick and after being tested, I was told I had cancer and it was serious. The doctor put me in the hospital and removed my left breast and the muscle under my left arm. That was March 16, 1981. After leaving the hospital, I was told, "From here it's a wait and see thing." The doctor put me under the care of the University Hospital at Little Rock.

After taking pain pills for the recovery of the cancer, I was again hooked on drugs. This led me back to alcohol. I stayed drunk and doped up for over a year, living the sickness of being a drug addict and alcoholic. I was constantly thinking, "Is this all that is left of my life?" I turned loose of my dear **Lord's** hand and now I was again doing it "John David's way."

I had been in and out of alcoholic hospitals during the first forty years of my life. Three times drying out and I now began to see I was back on that same "Old Road."

One morning, November the 2nd, 1982, as I was sitting on the side of my bed unable to tie my shoes due to weeks of drugging and drinking, I began to realize the condition I was in. I lay back on my bed and pretended to be asleep. My wife, Barbara, would be leaving shortly going to her insurance office. The children, David, Donna, and Doyen, had already left. Sitting on the side of my

The Great Reunion

bed, I began to look back at my past life, wondering through an altered doped up mind, "Would this demon of drugs and alcohol ever leave me?" With that thought in my warped mind, I got a pistol out of the dresser drawer. The demon voice inside me answered my question, "No, I will never leave you." At that I put the pistol to my head and pulled the trigger. I have no memory of anything from that morning until I woke up about twenty days later in a hospital room, paralyzed.

The first thought that came to my sobered mind was "Thank You, **Father**" for giving me one more chance to go to **Jesus** and to repent for the sins of which I was guilty. As I lay paralyzed in that hospital bed, I began to talk to my **Savior Jesus**. I said, "OK, it's all back in your hands, now. Do what is your 'will', but forgive me." That He did, right there in that hospital bed. I knew I was safe again and that I had my salvation back.

My precious wife Barbara has told me the doctors came to her during that time, and told her, "Today will probably be his last." The police came to her and gave the indication that she is the one who shot me. Again, I was putting my **God-given** wife through a torment of hell on earth. Help from **Jesus** carried her through it. The doctors kept warning her that I would be in a "vegetative state" and that she should put me in a nursing home. Barbara's answer was, "No, I'll take him home" and that is what she did.

For six months, I was confined to a wheel chair and going to therapy five days a week for six hours a day, learning to talk, to write, to move my arms and finally to walk again.

The **Holy Spirit** was encouraging me to get back into **God's** Holy Word, the Bible, and get the Holy Word back into my heart deeper than it had ever been before. "That I did."

I became ordained by the church and licensed by the Pulaski County Clerk, on March 5th, 1984. I was now doing what the **Lord** had wanted me to do all of my life. I was now His minister of His gospel. I would allow **God's** Holy Love and His Mercy and Grace to stay with me and be the number one priority for my life.

But remember, Satan, that Devil, is always and forever will be ready and very willing to tempt **God's** children. In my case, that's exactly what he did when he sent a man to me with a proposition of how much money he would pay me and what my great wealth would be after just one year. Would I go back into the drug trafficking with the Spanish Mafia? It would only be for one year.

At this time, I wanted to start a home for "troubled and homeless children". I thought to myself, this is the answer to my problems. I'll do this for one year and then I'll quit and put in the children's home. Oh, **God**! What a lie I had told myself.

The **Holy Spirit** actually spoke to me and said, "I'm not in this." I said, "We'll see you in one year." **God**, through the intercession of **Jesus,** has now forgiven me of this sin. Hallelujah!!

Now, by this time you may say, "No I don't believe God is willing to continually forgive a man who doesn't deserve to be forgiven." Well, as far as deserving, I didn't deserve to be forgiven the first time. And NO, **God's** mercy doesn't run out with His children. We must

The Great Reunion

remember as flesh and blood, we have very seldom had our mercy run out. Our mercy doesn't run out even on our own children. They can come and say, Daddy, Mother, please forgive me and we do. With our **God**, His mercy is not understandable for men to comprehend. Our love is not even a shadow of His love. Now, please don't misunderstand. **God** will not allow us to keep on rebelling against Him. We will have a payment for these rebellions against him, but He is always willing to forgive when we come to Him asking for His forgiveness and with the heart repenting and willing to change. Now, remember **God** knows your heart and your mind, right down to the smallest thought. He knows true repentance.

I began to do drug trafficking for an organization in 1991 and continued in it until September of 1992 with the thought in mind, "I will quit after this last trip." I was caught, and busted with 2000 pounds of marijuana in my warehouse in North Little Rock. All together, there were nine of us indicted on the charge of Conspiracy to distribute Marijuana. My wife and son Doyen were also

---

NLR man gets life sentence after

BY PATRICIA MANSON
Democrat-Gazette Federal Reporter

A man charged after a raid at a North Little Rock warehouse turned up a ton of marijuana was sentenced Friday to life in prison.

John David Whitehead was the last of nine defendants to be sentenced by Chief U.S. District Judge Stephen M. Reasoner.

Whitehead, of North Little Rock previously had pleaded guilty to six drug-related charges.

Reasoner imposed the sentence on Whitehead after determining that he was suffering from a mental disease or defect.

The sentence was the maximum Whitehead could have received.

The sentence also was provisional, meaning Reasoner could resentence Whitehead if he later is certified to be competent.

Any final sentence the judge later imposes could range from the minimum of 20 years to the maximum life

arrested and charged with "conspiracy", knowing what I was doing and not telling. My wife begged me all the time I was in it to stop this trafficking, "Please, stop this insane thing you are doing." Still in the end, she too, would have to pay.

On June 20th, I went in front of Federal Judge Reasoner and pled guilty to all five charges I had been charged with. It was a total surprise to everyone, even my own lawyer. The other eight would go to trial. After spending four hundred and thirty one days in different Arkansas County and City jails, I was brought back into court on July 15th and at that time I was sentenced to a LIFE sentence. Normally, the court gives no more than four months maximum after a defendant has entered a plea of guilty. But, in my case, I do believe that Judge Reasoner had his mind made up from the very first. I had shocked the court by pleading without warning. Now, it's my belief that Judge Reasoner took this 431 days from the time I pled guilty until he sentenced me to do a pre-sentencing investigation that would for sure stick with

---

Arkansas Democrat 🐘 Gazette

ton of 'pot' found at warehouse

term Whitehead received Friday.

Reasoner in January sentenced eight other people in the case to terms ranging up to 10 years and four months. Those sentenced included Whitehead's wife, Barbara, and the couple's son, Doyen Floyd Whitehead.

Reasoner also forfeited to the government all interest the defendants had in Val-Care Environmental Services Inc.

Law enforcement officials said the company, which purportedly disposed of medical waste, was a front to disguise the movement of marijuana from southern Texas to Arkansas and then to major urban areas in the northern part of the country.

The marijuana was stored in boxes marked "medical waste" until it could be repackaged for shipment, officials said.

Law enforcement officials at that time said it was the largest marijuana seizure in North Little Rock history.

the sentence he was going to give me. I do honestly believe I saw hate in the Judge's eyes this day.

You see, I had come to the point where I could not do as I had done in 1973, plead innocent and take the stand under oath and again lie like a dog. I just couldn't do it. So to myself, I said, "You are guilty, plead that way." I took the life sentence I was now carrying and was shipped by Federal Marshals to Rochester, Minnesota, to the Federal Prison to start serving my time.

A Road That Won't Travel

Chapter 3

When I arrived at the federal prison in Minnesota, I was put into Building Number One, known as the "Nut House". Building One, in my opinion is the most dangerous building in the Federal Prison System. There are approximately eighty inmates who live in that building, seventy of which are stone-nut's-crazy. If I were to mention just a few of the men by name who are housed there, anyone who watches the news on TV or reads the newspapers would say "I remember them."

I sat in my cell for the first year doing absolutely nothing. Even my food trays were brought in to me. Many times, I would listen as my very precious nurse would ask, "John David, would you like a Bible to read?" to which, I would answer "No". My thoughts were no longer on my **Master** and my **Lord** and **Savior Jesus**." Instead, I thought of my precious wife and son; how that for just knowing of my actions they both had been given sentences of ten years each. They were both now in prison doing that time and it was eating me alive.

One day as my nurse stood in my cell talking to me, I said, "Will you please get me a Bible? This hate I have for myself is killing me." I got back into the precious Holy Word and read it for a year.

After reading **God's** Holy Word and praying for a full year, one night, the **Holy Spirit** was within my soul so strong, I started praying. I said, "**God**, through your Son **Jesus** and His blood that He spilt at Calvary, I know you are willing to forgive me. Now, tell me how to forgive myself."

The Great Reunion

```
UNITED STATES DEPARTMENT OF JUSTICE
FEDERAL BUREAU OF PRISONS
                        PROGRESS REPORT

         FMC, Rochester, MN                      10-03-1996
             INSTITUTION                           DATE
Inmate Reviewed:
    [signature: John Whitehead]    10-15-96    [signature]
      Inmate's Signature             Date       Staff Signature
```

1. Type of Progress Report:

   Initial: __XX__   Statutory Interim: _____   Pre-Release: _____

   Transfer: _____   Biennial: __XX__   Other (specify): _____

2. Name	3. Register Number	4. Age (DOB)
WHITEHEAD, John David	19453-009	61 (05-13-1935)

5. Present Security/Custody Level

   HIGH Security/IN Custody

6. Offense/Violator Offense

   Conspiracy to Distribute Marijuana

7. Sentence

   Life; §244 Hospitalization and Treatment.

8. Sentence Began	9. Months Served - Jail Credit	10. Days GCT/or GT/SGT
07-15-1994	27 months + 431 days JCT	Not Applicable
11. Days FSGT/WSGT/DGCT	12. Projected Release	13. Last USPC Action
Not Applicable	Life	Not Eligible

14. Detainers/Pending Charges

    None Known

15. Codefendants

    Barbara Whitehead, Samuel Mendez, Raul Cruz, Marco Antonio Lopez, Ricky Lynn Wallis, Doyen Floyd Whitehead, Jimmy Don Winemiller, Jr., and Keith Gunter

Distribution: Inmate File
                U.S. Probation Office
                Parole Commission Regional Office (If applicable)
                Inmate

Federal Prison Progress Report

All that night the **Holy Ghost** bloomed with the love of **God** within my soul. As I showered the next morning, I began to praise **God** and thank Him through His **Holy Spirit**. I did not hate myself any longer. The **Holy Spirit** had set me free. Once again, I had the three **Holy Ones** back together within me. I was free indeed. Hallelujah!!!

My staff team, which consisted of approximately eight people had been calling me on "call out" to come and meet with them every four to six months for the two years I had been there. At the last progress report, I had been asked by one of the team members, "Mr. Whitehead, what are you going to do about this life sentence?" I said, "Ms. Miller, I am not going to do nothing. I have messed up my family's life and my own enough. So you are going to have to live with me for the rest of my life, as long as I live." At that, Ms Miller said, "We thought that might be your answer before we asked. But, we don't think you should have a life sentence. We don't think at the time you were sentenced you were competent and should not have been sentenced." Then Ms. Miller said, "If you will sign the proper papers, we have decided we will intervene for you with the court." I agreed and signed the papers. NEVER have I seen this or even heard of this being done for one single man, never before or since.

§   §   §

October the 7th, 1997, I was awakened at 3:00 AM by the staff nurse and told to get up. "You are to be in court at 9:00 AM this morning." I was so confused that I asked, "What time is it now?" The nurse said, "It's 3:00 AM, but there are Federal Marshals waiting in the front lobby for you, to take you to the airport. There is a Lear Jet waiting to fly you to Little Rock, so get dressed quickly. Sure enough, at 9:00 AM that morning I was sitting at a table in the courtroom with a new court-appointed lawyer, Jennifer Horan. At 9:00 AM, Judge Reasoner entered the courtroom. I was shocked when I saw his face. It was a face full of compassion, not the hate I saw when he first sentenced me. I truly believe as he started questioning me, he saw a broken repentant man. I believe he saw remorse all over me for the sin I had committed against my country and he could see great sorrow. After he had talked with me, he spoke with Ms. Jennifer and told her he had thought in his mind to cut my sentence from life down to twenty years. Then he said, "But now that you have asked me to cut it down to fourteen years, I'm just going to do that." As he fumbled through papers he had in front of him, he said, "I see where I sentenced, Raul Cruz, the second in command, to fourteen years, and I don't want Raul Cruz to have as much time as Mr. Whitehead, so I will cut Raul Cruz's time down to thirteen years. So Raul Cruz got a year cut off his own sentence and wasn't even in court. I walked out of the court with a fourteen-year sentence. **God's Holy Spirit** had taken charge of the things that happened in the hour that I was in court. My precious wife was fined $17,500, my son $5,000, and each of the other six were fined $1,000. I was not fined one dollar. I will always believe the **Holy Spirit** had dumbfounded Judge Reasoner's mind and he completely forgot to fine me. I was brought back to Rochester Prison to do the rest of my time . . . . . again, "Building One."

At the next team meeting, which was about three weeks after my returning from court, I asked the team would they help me get transferred closer to Little Rock; because in the three years I had been at Rochester, I had not had a single visit. The team leader said, "We know that and we are even now in the process of getting your "Extremely High" security level lowered to a "medium" level, so we can do that. Three months later I was cleared for Medium Level Security, and I was transferred to Fort Worth Medical Center, at Fort Worth, Texas.

At this time I was taking medication for my mind. I was diagnosed several years ago as having severe dementia. This was caused at the time I shot myself. Mayo Clinic had looked at my injury during the time I was at Rochester Prison and they determined that the bullet that was now lodged in my brain could not be removed. The doctors in Little Rock had determined the same thing. This dementia was getting worse, and times would come when I was completely lost. I was also hurting badly with headaches.

One day a notice was put on the bulletin board that the ministry of Gloria Copeland was coming to the prison the following Sunday. I thought to myself, I'll go and hear her. She preached her sermon that Sunday morning with a dynamite power of the **Holy Spirit**. After the close of the sermon, Sister Copeland gave an altar call, telling the men, if anyone had a need that needs to be met, that **Jesus** is willing to take care of that need right now, "'Come forth." I knew that was for me. So I said to my precious **Holy Spirit**, "Take me forth, that I may be prayed for at this minute". He did! As I approached the altar, I told Sister Copeland, "My mind needs to be healed." At that, she placed her hand on my forehead and said, "Be Whole" and walked away. As I got back to my unit, I went to bed early that night thinking to myself, "**Lord**, that wasn't very much of a prayer that Sister Copeland prayed for me." At that time I heard my Holy Spirit say, "It was enough for me." I knew then I was healed.

For the next six weeks, it was like walking out of a fog into sunshine. My mind was now, as the saying goes, clear as a bell. I was put "on call" out to come to my doctor's office at the hospital. That I did and as I walked in he began to say to me, "Whitehead, I see where you have not been taking your medication for six weeks." I answered, "Doctor, I have been healed." He said, "You cannot be healed of Dementia. All there is for that is to take your medication and that's what you have got to do!" I said, "I have been healed by the stripes of **Jesus**. I don't have Dementia any more and I will not take any medication." At that he told me, "If you don't take your medication, I will put you on transfer." I knew what that meant, "Diesel Therapy" and I also knew I would be living on the "Edge of Hell" for as long as this lasted.

§ § §

Here is a list of the prisons I have spent time in during my ten years of confinement. The times of being isolated and put in the hole, are due to my unstable mental condition.

(1.) El Reno, Oklahoma-Arkansas: 70 days in the hole

(2.) Springfield, Mo. Building Ten: 120 days in isolation

(3.) Different city, county jails in Ark.: 431 days

(4.) Texarkana, Texas: 20 days spent in the hole

(5.) Seogoville, Texas: 6 days spent in the hole

(6.) Rochester, Minnesota: 4 years, Building "Number 1"

(7.) Memphis, Tenn.: 3 months in open population

(8.) Forest City, Ark: 3 months of constant escort

(9.) Devens, Mass.: 1 year - The "Hell Hole"

(10.) Fort Worth, Texas: 4 years, Medical Center.

    I was transferred from one place to another from 1999 until 2001. This was the diesel therapy I was talking about. Two years of misery and then I was transferred back to the Fort Worth Medical Center. I started out my prison transferring from Fort Worth to Memphis. This was pretty much of a "Laid Back Prison" where all you had to do was keep your nose clean and stay out of trouble.
    I was there three months, and then one night they woke me up and I was told "Get yourself ready, you are being transferred." I said, "Tonight?" and they said "Yes,

tonight." The next day I was at the Federal Prison in Forrest City, Arkansas. After being interviewed by the prison doctor and the doctor calling the security officer into her office, I was told by the security officer that the doctor had recommended that I be given inmate security companionship to escort me, for security reasons. I laughed and said, "Whatever." This would be what I called the "Fun House." It would be the best, easiest time I had in prison, but it only lasted three months. Then one morning I was told, by the security officer to get ready, we were going on a trip. As we got to the local airport, I was put aboard a Lear Jet and three hours later I was at the Rochester, Minnesota airport. There to meet me was my favorite precious nurse with a security officer. I was, as I told her, "back home." She laughed and they took me back to "Building One." This time, I was only there three months and was transferred to Devens, Massachusetts by Lear Jet. I knew from the very first hour at the Devens prison, this was going to be a Hell Hole, and it turned out worse than what I had thought or ever imagined. How I managed to spend one year there without being reprimanded or put on disciplinary report is beyond me. Without the leading of the **Holy Spirit**, I could not.

In October of 2000, I was sent back to Fort Worth Medical Center. The first person I saw at the hospital was my old doctor. He did recognize me and I said to him, "Well, my diesel therapy is over. Then I said, "No, I haven't taken a single pill since I last saw you." He said, "If after all this time and you still recognize me, it may be that your Dementia is healed."

My first thought upon getting settled back in was to join the Hospice Volunteer Program, a program designed to help take care of Hospice patients who have been diagnosed by the doctor to have less than six months to live. I would be reading, writing letters, and helping with their personal needs and most important of all, reading and explaining what is **God's** plan for their Salvation – the Rescue from Great Danger.

Very recently, I was able, to be used by **God's Holy Spirit** in bringing a friend of mine to the Throne of Grace, where he repented and received **Jesus** as his **Lord and Savior**. He died the very next day. Thank **God**, he died saved.

Then soon I was allowed to join the Drug Abuse Program, which meant sometime in 2003, latter part of the year, I would have done my time and would be set free.

The Great Reunion

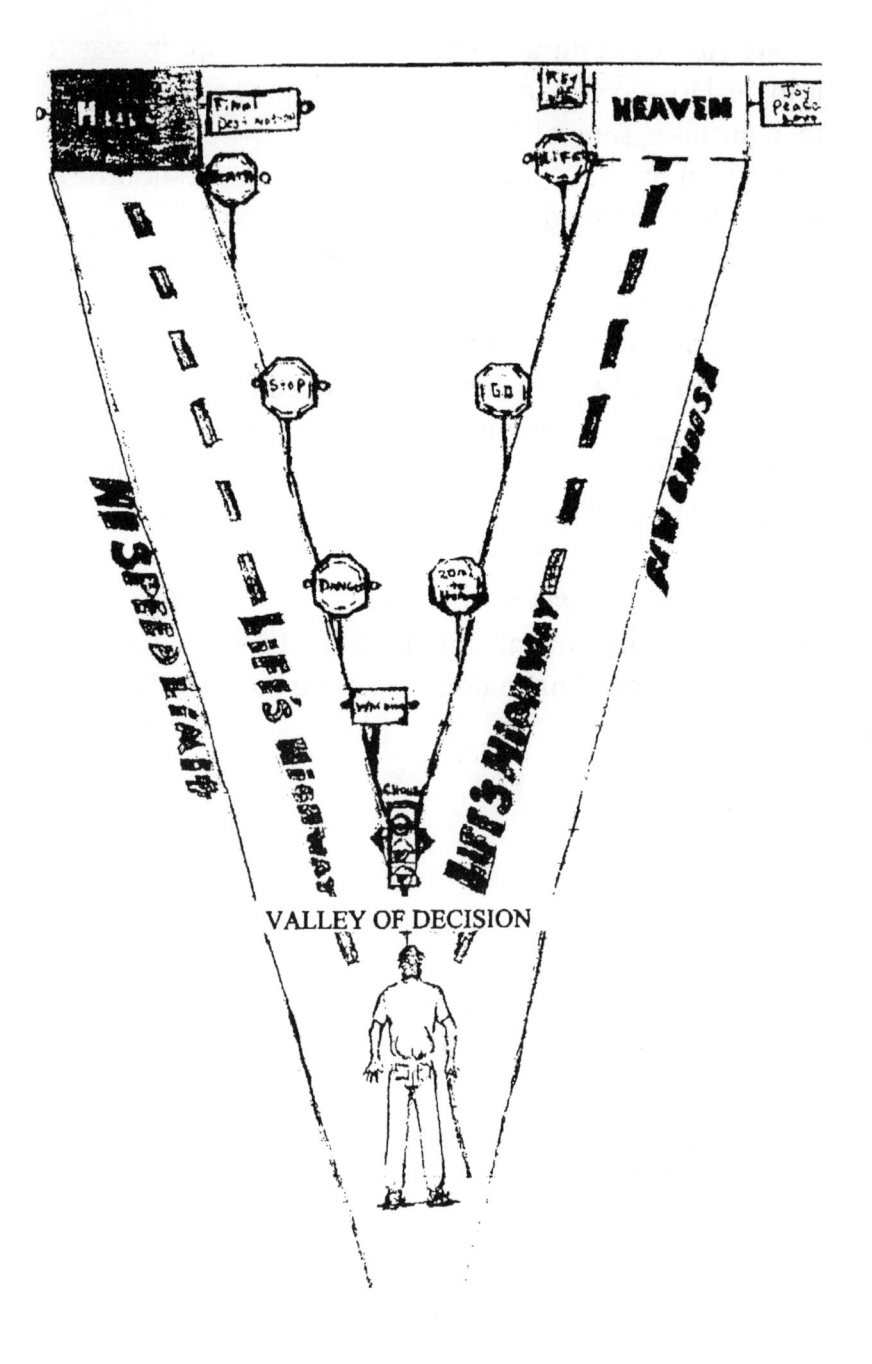

VALLEY OF DECISION

Chapter 4

My hope and desire is to be allowed to come into your churches, schools, colleges, even stadiums, and declare to your young people that "THE ROAD OF DRUGS AND ALCOHOL" will not travel!!!

I want to tell your young people, "If you are on this road "GET OFF" it won't work, no matter how hard you may try, IT JUST WON'T WORK." I know, I was on it for fifty years.

Today as I write this book, I have one dollar and seventy four cents in my account. I have a mountain of scars of sickness, lonesomeness, and, yes, even insanity; all caused by this road I have traveled. Please don't travel it. It won't work.

In closing, let me tell you, I have been on "highs" of all kinds from every kind of drug. I have been on all kinds of highs from alcohol. But the highest of all highs, was when I got high on the love of **God** and the Blood of **Jesus** with the leading of the **Holy Ghost**. This is an everlasting, eternal, high that **Jesus** is right now offering you. It's a Freeway that will bring you to heaven and life forevermore. THANK **GOD**, I AM NOW TRAVELING ON THAT VERY FREEWAY TO HEAVEN!

Won't you come travel it, too?

God loves you and so do I . . .

John David Whitehead
Servant for **Jesus Christ** and friend of the **Masters**

The Great Reunion

Five Steps to Salvation

(RESCUE FROM GREAT DANGER)   *EVERLASTING LIFE*

(1) (JOHN 3:16) FOR **GOD** SO LOVED THE WORLD, THAT HE GAVE HIS ONLY BEGOTTEN SON, THAT WHOSOEVER BELIEVETH IN **HIM** SHOULD NOT PERISH, BUT HAVE EVERLASTING LIFE.

(2) (JOHN 14:6) **JESUS** SAITH UNTO HIM, I AM THE WAY, THE TRUTH, AND THE LIFE: NO MAN COMETH UNTO **THE FATHER**, BUT BY ME.

(3) (ACTS 2:21) AND IT SHALL COME TO PASS, THAT WHOSOEVER SHALL CALL ON THE NAME OF THE **LORD** SHALL BE SAVED.

(4) (ROMANS 10:9) THAT IF THOU SHALT CONFESS WITH THY MOUTH TO THE **LORD JESUS** AND SHALT BELIEVE IN THINE HEART THAT **GOD** HATH RAISED **HIM** FROM THE DEAD, THOU SHALT BE SAVED.

(5) (EPHESIANS 2:8) FOR BY GRACE ARE YOU SAVED THROUGH FAITH; AND THAT NOT OF YOURSELVES: IT IS THE GIFT OF **GOD**.

BE BAPTIZED, READ THE BIBLE, AND GO TO THE CHURCH OF YOUR CHOICE.

The Great Reunion

RIVER ROAD UNDENOMINATIONAL CHURCH

DATE: 3-5-84

TO WHOM IT MAY CONCERN:

CERTIFICATION OF ORDINATION

We the undersigned, hereby certify that, upon the recommendation of the members of the River Road Undenominational Church which had full and sufficient opportunity for judging his/her gifts and after satisfactory examination by us in regard to his/her Christian Experience, call to the ministry, and view of Bible Doctrine, JOHN DAVID WHITEHEAD was solemnly and publicly ordained to the work of the Gospel Ministry by the authority of the River Road Undenominational Church at Redfield, Arkansas on this 4th day of March, 1984.

Earl Thomas
Pastor

James B. Aaron
Trustee

Martha Carnical
Secretary/Treasurer

John David Whitehead
Minister of Certification

FILED: March 5, 1984
RECORDED: March 5, 1984
SHIRLEY D. SMITH, COUNTY CLERK
RECORDED BY: Sherry King, Deputy Clerk

The Great Reunion

NOTES

God Bless You All As You Read This Book

Normally this page is reserved for the reader's notes and comments when reading a book such as this, but Mr. Whitehead has graciously asked me to write something here.

Remembering from studying the word that our Father chooses in advance those who He knows can and will fulfill His calling. He does allow us to be put through the fire and tempered as fine steel. He also knows those who will stand the heat and who can deliver the message. **God** knows the best examples are those who have had the experience. He gives Satan a short leash at times, but He always knows what the outcome will be.

I find in Mr. Whitehead a man of sincerity and much courage. Having learned the lessons the hard way, he would like to prevent as many young people as he can from making the same mistakes as he did.

His message comes direct from the heart and **God** alone knows the value of that.

Take this little book and read it with your children and then listen to him speak. You will hear truth as few have heard it and, if you take to heart his words, you will save many young lives from the pains of hell and worse, while they yet live, and give them a home in heaven when they have gone on.

We are privileged to assist in this much needed ministry. Thank you, *John David* and **God** Bless you in His service.

-- *Wanda Wilson*

The Great Reunion

A Note from the Author

I wish I could describe what heaven looks like, but the only thing I can do is give you some scriptures that tell of it. Psalms 11:4 say's that the **Lord** is in His holy temple. The **Lord's** throne is in heaven.

Now try to imagine, this is the very **God** who will be having this great reunion that this book, <u>The Great Reunion</u>, is speaking of to you.

The awesomeness of heaven is so far above man's imagination that even **Jesus** had to speak in parables to give them the understanding of heaven as He explained to His disciples about the greatness of heaven. Read (Matthew 18:2-3-4) and **Jesus** called a little child unto Him and set him in the midst of them. And said, "Verily I say unto you, except ye be converted, and become as little children, ye shall not enter into the Kingdom of Heaven. Whosoever, therefore, shall humble himself as this little child, the same is greatest in the Kingdom of Heaven".

This is **Jesus** the Master of your Salvation. (Rescue from Great Danger.) Now, He is, wanting to sign your own personal invitation to come to this "Great Reunion" that **God** the **Father** is going to have; to be signed with the Blood of **Jesus**. Accept and receive it today. Tomorrow may be too late.

Has there not been enough wasted years?

Always remember: **God** loves you . . . and so do I.

-- John David Whitehead

Dear Reader,

This Letter of Appreciation is just one reason for my writing this book and for my entire ministry. It's to tell the young people who have one foot in prison and the other one on unholy ground that the **"Life Against God"** and against men's laws is a road that won't travel. It just **will not** work.

I thank **"God Almighty"** that I am no longer traveling that road anymore. I am now on a freeway that will lead to heaven where I will personally see and talk with the One who gave His life for me, who is **"Jesus Christ"**.

Many thanks to you, Ms. Denise Pearson, my sister in **"Christ Jesus"**, for giving me the opportunity to come and speak to the young people in the Juvenile Detention Center in Little Rock, Arkansas.

This is what it is all about.

John David Whitehead
John David Whitehead

A Road That Won't Travel

Pulaski County

Administrative Services
Juvenile Detention Center

3001 West Roosevelt
Little Rock, AR 72204
501-340-6697 Phone
501-340-6888 Fax

COUNT PULASKI

Mr. and Mrs. Whitehead
J.D.W. Ministry
#72 Jo Jo Lane
N.L.R. AR 72117

Dear Mr. and Mrs. Whitehead,

CITIES
ALEXANDER
CAMMACK VILLAGE
JACKSONVILLE
LITTLE ROCK
MAUMELLE
NORTH LITTLE ROCK
SHERWOOD
WRIGHTSVILLE

UNINCORPORATED AREA
600 SQUARE MILES

On behalf of the Pulaski County Juvenile Detention Center, I would like to extend our sincere appreciation for the motivational presentation that you delivered to our youth on August 26, 2004. It is the mission of the center not only to provide for the basic needs of the juveniles, but also to ensure a rehabilitative environment that entails emotional, psychological, religious and educational support. Your presentation touched all of these areas and certainly helped us to achieve our programming goals.

Each speaker that comes to the detention center has a unique style of presenting. It is always interesting to watch and see how the kids respond to the speaker and his/her presentation. I believe our children could feel the genuine concern you have in your hearts for them and could see that your intentions to help them were sincere. Because you have both walked in their shoes and lived their lives, it provided a powerful connection to their own lives and they listened not only with their ears but also with their hearts. Thank you for having the courage to share the triumphs and tragedies of your own journeys through life. The kids really enjoyed receiving copies of your book, The Great Reunion. I know many of them read the book as I heard them making comments to one another about it. It is not often they receive gifts and I am sure they will treasure it and maybe even use it as a resource in troubled times.

I hope your experience was a positive one and that you both will consider coming back again in the future to reach many more of our youth. We are looking forward to your return visit to detention to minister through music on November 12, 2004. May God continue to bless you in your efforts to reach out to the youth of our community and maybe help prevent some of them from going down the long road it took for you before you found hope and healing.

MILITARY BASES
LRAFB
CAMP ROBINSON

Sincerely,

T. Denise Pearson
PCJDC Counselor

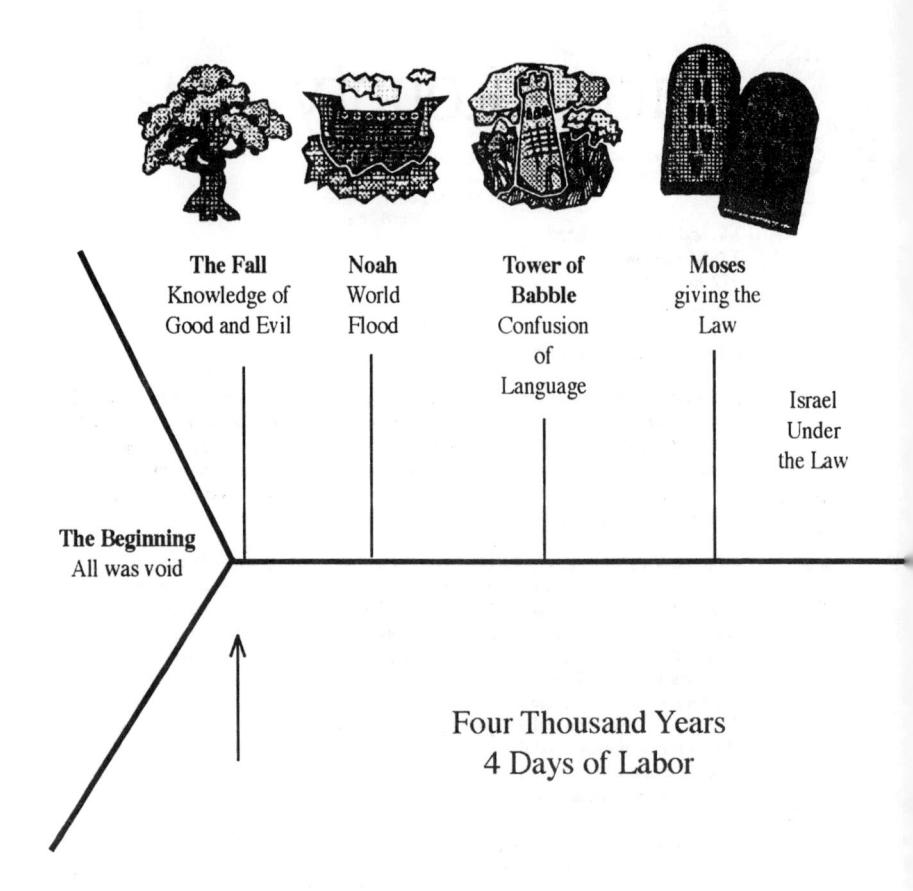

The Great Reunion

The Fall
Knowledge of
Good and Evil

Noah
World
Flood

**Tower of
Babble**
Confusion
of
Language

Moses
giving the
Law

Israel
Under
the Law

The Beginning
All was void

Four Thousand Years
4 Days of Labor

A Road That Won't Travel

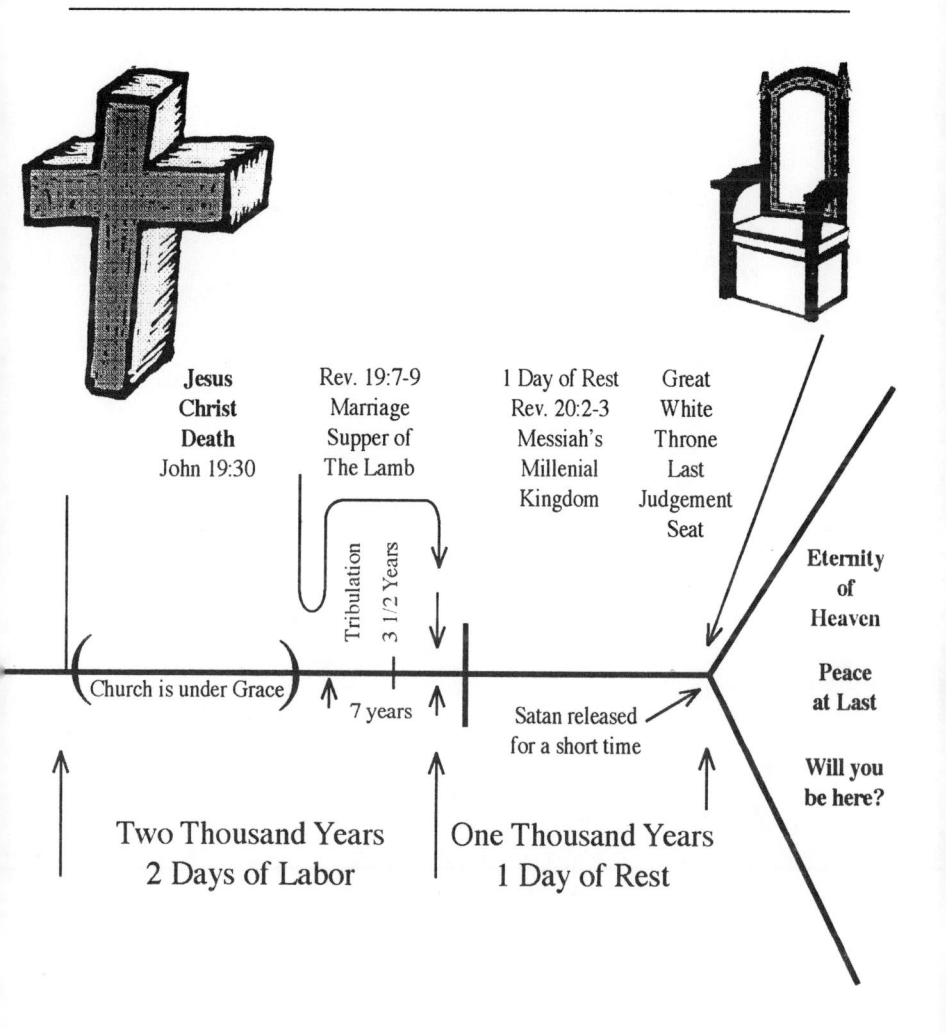

Jesus Christ Death
John 19:30

Rev. 19:7-9
Marriage Supper of The Lamb

1 Day of Rest
Rev. 20:2-3
Messiah's Millenial Kingdom

Great White Throne Last Judgement Seat

Tribulation 3 1/2 Years

(Church is under Grace)

7 years

Satan released for a short time

Eternity of Heaven

Peace at Last

Will you be here?

Two Thousand Years
2 Days of Labor

One Thousand Years
1 Day of Rest

The Great Reunion

A Road That Won't Travel

Order Form

The Great Reunion   **$8.99 US**

plus $3.01 each for shipping and handling charges.
(Total $12.00 each US)

Enclosed is my check for $_____ for ___ copies.
Please send my books to:

Name: _____

Street Address: _____

City, ST & Zip: _____

Also enclosed is my gift of $_____ to help support the efforts to spread the gospel of "Jesus". *All donations are Tax Deductable*

John David Whitehead

Send Form with your check to:

"J.D.W. Ministry of Jesus Christ"
P.O. Box 17881
North Little Rock, Arkansas 72117
(501) 961-1611

Order form #I-122

The Great Reunion